yoga for the
brain

DAWN DiPRINCE   CHERYL MILLER THURSTON

COTTONWOOD PRESS, INC.

Requests for special permission should be addressed to:

Cottonwood Press, Inc.
109-B Cameron Drive
Fort Collins, Colorado 80525

Email: cottonwood@cottonwoodpress.com
Phone: 1-800-864-4297
Fax: 970-204-0761
www.cottonwoodpress.com

ISBN 1-877673-71-4

Printed in the United States of America

Cover illustration by Larry Nolte

Table of Contents

Introduction

Writing is great exercise for the brain. The very act of transforming thoughts and ideas into words on paper helps a person stretch all kinds of mind muscles. It helps clarify thinking. It forces creativity. It builds strength.

Writing helps people look at their ideas through the eyes of an audience, whether real or imagined. It helps them sharpen their thinking as they try to communicate in words alone, without the help of a certain tone of voice, a raised eyebrow, or a wink.

Writing helps build strong minds, but it also helps keep minds young. Just as bodies stay strong with exercise, minds are more likely to stay strong with the exercise of examining, communicating, and creating, through writing.

For individuals to use on their own, or for teachers to use with students.
Yoga for the Brain includes a variety of writing exercises, from silly to serious, from straightforward to creative, from observational to reflective. Some are personal, some objective. There are exercises for every day of the year, but feel free to skip around. If one idea doesn't appeal to you, try another. If you are using the exercises with students, you will find there are a variety of lengths—exercises that can be done in just a minute or two, as well as longer exercises that might take several class periods to complete.

Whatever you do, however you use the book, take time to enjoy what you are doing. If you are writing for yourself, keep your materials all together, perhaps in a loose leaf notebook so that you can add and eliminate pages as necessary. A computer file is a lifesaver, but you may want to print out what you write. Those hard copies will often allow you to observe something that you will never quite see on the screen, whether it's a spelling mistake, a lapse in logic, a paragraph that is especially persuasive, or a great metaphor you hadn't appreciated before.

If you are using the exercises with students, we strongly encourage you not to grade them—or at the very least, not all of them. You might simply give credit for completing the assignments, perhaps letting students themselves choose three different activities to be graded over the course of the semester. The value of the exercises is in the doing. Yes, grammar, punctuation, and other conventions are important. But they aren't always important every step of the way. In fact, paying too much attention to mechanics early on can actually hamper progress.

"Real world" writing projects. Something both of us have come to value is the effectiveness of what we call "real world" projects in helping people learn. A few years ago, someone we know was completing, half-heartedly, the tutorials for a difficult computer program. She wasn't making much progress. Suddenly, an employee was hospitalized at a time when the company had a deadline. Our friend had to finish the project, using the new computer program. In a few days, she learned more than she had in the previous year, and in no time was fairly adept. Having a real-world goal forced her to become serious.

Similarly, we both have noticed improvement in writing when our students are working on a real product to share with someone other than the teacher. For example, individuals become much more serious writers when they are completing autobiographies as keepsakes for their families. If students are writing a skit to be performed in front of the class, they work much harder than on assignments that are shared only with the teacher. People working on their resumés for a job application suddenly are much more interested in spelling and punctuation than they are when completing routine class assignments.

Because of the "real-world" effect on people, we encourage individuals using *Yoga for the Brain* to choose a real-world writing project that has meaning for them. We have provided a wide variety of ideas, starting on page 115, but readers will likely have many other ideas as well.

We encourage you to use *Yoga for the Brain* as it was intended—as exercise. Like yoga, it can be exercise you enjoy!

Dawn DiPrince and Cheryl Miller Thurston.

365 Writing Prompts

1. **Introduce yourself,** using one *true* detail and one *untrue* detail about you or your life. As you write, try to make both the true and untrue details sound equally believable.

2. **Take the untrue detail you wrote about and elaborate.** Expand. Fill in details. If you wrote that you once played a role in a television commercial, tell how you got the role, how you felt about the product, who you met filming the commercial, etc.

3. **Take the true detail you wrote about, and turn it into fiction.** Add details that are false. For example, if you wrote that you have red hair, you might add untrue details about how you dye it every week because the natural color is an unhealthy looking blondish-green, and you have to keep dying it because otherwise you don't resemble the picture on your driver license.

4. **All writing is truth, and all writing is fiction.** Is that true? How is that possible? Explore some possibilities. (You may wish to look over and think about your answers to #1-3 first.)

5. **Describe yourself as you think you looked**—or know you looked—on your very first day of kindergarten or first grade. What were you wearing? Did you choose your clothes, or did someone else? How did you feel? Did it show on your face or in your actions?

6. **Write about a person who has touched your life** in some small but meaningful way. Perhaps it was a kind neighbor, a forgiving policeman, a friend who stuck up for you when someone was being mean. What did that person do—or not do—that affected you?

7. **Clarissa and Elaina can't stand each other.** Describe the meeting they are both attending. Let us know they can't stand each other without *telling* us they can't stand each other.

8.

Describe a small memory that involves someone older than you. Perhaps it's your mother standing at the kitchen counter peeling potatoes or your grandfather showing you how to start a lawn mower. Describe that small memory, creating a snapshot in time. Use details from all five senses—smell, sight, touch, hearing, taste. (If you can't remember details from all of them, create details that very well *might* have been true.)

---

9. **It has been suggested that the reason so many people today participate in extreme sports** is because life itself doesn't offer the physical challenges of "the olden days." Today we don't travel across the country in covered wagons or plow fields by hand or weave our own cloth for clothing. Some even say the lack of physical challenge helps explain the popularity of tattoos, body piercing, and dangerous drugs. Life is easy, so we create our own challenges.

What do you think of this notion? Do you think we create our own challenges? Why or why not? Explain.

10. If you had to describe yourself as a **cat person** or a **dog person**, which would it be? Why?

11. If you had to describe yourself as a **fish person** or a **bird person**, which would it be? Why?

12. **What would a corporate-style logo for YOU look like?** What color would it be? What would it symbolize about you? Draw your logo and explain its significance.

13. **Which one of these "m" words** best describes you: *melancholy, morose, morbid, malleable, macho, meek, maniacal, miserable* or *merry?* Explain.

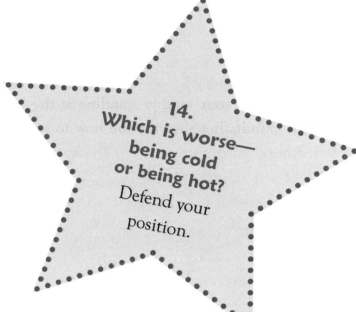

14. Which is worse—being cold or being hot? Defend your position.

15. **Apart from anything in your personal life, what saddens you?** Is it something in the news? Something you observe every day on your way to work or school? Explain.

16. **CTRL-Z, in most computer programs,** allows you to undo your last action. Have you ever found yourself wishing you had a CTRL-Z in other aspects of your life? What if the lawn mower had a CTRL-Z, so you could undo hitting the rock that flew into the window? What if your mouth had a CTRL-Z, so that you could undo unkind words?

   What other uses can you think of for a CTRL-Z outside the world of the computer?

17. **Describe the joy of bare feet.** Make bare feet sound so desirable that we will all want to go strip off our shoes and socks.

18. **Someone in the house across the street from you** has been raising and lowering the blinds constantly for about an hour. Write an explanation of this strange behavior.

20. **What book character** do you resemble, at least in some way? Explain.

19.
You are at a job interview. Your job test, odd as it may seem, is this:

In one paragraph, make mashed potatoes exciting.

What will you say?

21. **The word *hero* is used a lot today.** It has been used to describe a dog that barks to wake up its owner when it smells smoke, a rich person who donates money to a cause, a teenager who dies in a car accident, a father who coaches his son's soccer league, a soldier injured in war, a rock star, and a child who turns in a lost wallet. Some say that the term is used far too loosely and has little meaning. Still others complain that there just aren't any heroes left in our world today. How do you feel about heroes? What makes a hero? Do you know any heroes? Explain.

22.
In a small way, a big way, or many ways, how do you hope you are like your mother?

23.
In a small way, a big way, or many ways, how do you hope you are like your father?

24. Describe three teeny-tiny "downers" that annoy you.
Downers are very personal. They are the little aggravations of life, not the big ones. Losing your wallet or being in a bike accident is not a teeny-tiny downer. A teeny-tiny downer is that little ball of hard lotion that forms at the spout of a bottle of hand lotion and comes out in a hard blob when you squirt lotion onto your hands.

25. Describe three teeny-tiny "uppers" in your life. Teeny-tiny uppers are very personal. They are little pleasures that you notice only fleetingly, if at all. Winning the lottery or falling in love is not a teeny-tiny upper. A teeny-tiny upper is that satisfying little "bling" sound you hear on your computer when you've got mail.

26. Suppose you were able to choose the family you were born into—and the family you actually wound up with in real life was not available. What kind of family would you choose? Why?

27. Which is best—city life, life in the suburbs, or life in the country? Explain.

28.
Here's the title of a book:

The Universe Is Square.

Write a blurb describing the book for the book jacket or back cover.

29.
There is another book called *The Universe Is Square,* on an entirely different subject for an entirely different audience. The blurb you wrote for Item #28 won't work, of course. Write the blurb for this second book.

30.

Have you ever felt frustrated trying to follow unclear instructions? You might have been filling out a government form, completing a homework assignment, or trying to install a piece of computer equipment, for example. Sometimes instructions are confusing because the sentences are needlessly long and complex. Sometimes they are filled with terminology that may not be at all clear to the reader. Sometimes they are simply inaccurate or not well-written.

Imagine a twisted or demented "instructions writer" who actually receives pleasure out of trying to make instructions as confusing as possible. Then imagine that *you* are that twisted writer.

Below are some instructions. Rewrite them to make them as confusing as possible. Do not change what needs to be done. Just make what to do *much* harder to figure out.

• Write your name in the top right corner of the page, followed by your age.

• Write your address under your name.

• Write your home phone number in the top left corner of the page, followed by your cell phone number, if you have one.

• In one paragraph, explain why you are perfect for the position of head doughnut fryer. Do not exceed 100 words.

• Sign your name at the bottom of the page.

• Give your paper to the receptionist at the front desk.

31.
Write ten comparisons,
each comparing a
fictional person to a
household appliance.

32. **During the Industrial Revolution,** textile workers in England
destroyed factory equipment to protest labor-saving technology. They
claimed to be following the example of a man named Ned Ludd. Today, a
"Luddite" is a person who fears or hates technology. Luddites today
believe that technology is doing more harm than good in our society.

   Regardless of what you personally believe, explain why the Luddites
are right.

33. **Now, regardless of what you personally believe,** explain why
the Luddites are wrong. What small improvement in our modern world
do you appreciate?

34. **Create at least three more interesting ways** to say, "Her face is
an open book."

35. **If you played in a band,** what would you play? What kind of band would it be? Explain. (If you already play in a band, what instrument would you choose if you couldn't play the one you currently play?)

36. **Write a letter of apology,** without using the words *sorry* or *apologize*.

38. **Summarize a movie you like,** in 50 words or less, telling just the basic plot of the story.

    For example, here is *The Sound of Music* in 50 words or less:

    Rich Austrian hires nun-turned-governess as nanny to unruly children. Children are mean. Nanny shapes them up. Children learn to love nanny. Nanny learns to love children. Man learns to loves nanny. Nanny learns to love man. Nazis interfere. Man and nanny and children play trick and escape over the Alps.

> **37.**
> Write a story or paragraph that includes the following words:
>
> **airplane, pigeon, fiddle, battery, charger, Venus.**

39. **Write five sentences with unexpected verbs.** Here are a couple of examples:

    • *The CEO of the company looked at the board members and giggled.*
    • *The weightlifter skipped into the arena.*

> **40.**
> **Describe something you feel very, very strongly about.**
> Explain one of the reasons you feel the way you do.

41. Describe a mystery that really bothers you. Did someone once disappear in your town, never to be found again? Do you wonder what on earth your aunt could possibly see in her second husband? Do you wonder how sponsors of 100-mile races ever get even one person to enter? Did someone you know ever predict something would happen before it actually did? Describe a mystery, large or small.

42. What's right about this country? You have only 100 words, so use them wisely.

43. What's wrong with this country? You have only 100 words, so use them wisely.

44. Here's a real brain stretch. What does your brain look like inside, from a decorator's point of view? (Remember—think creatively here!) Are there windows? Curtains? If so, what kind? What colors do you see? How is the brain arranged—neat little stacks, spaghetti-like piles, or…? How does this décor reflect your personality?

45. Can numbers have special powers? Is there something magical about the number *3*? Is there any truth to the superstition that *13* is unlucky? Are there any numbers that have special significance in your life? Discuss.

46. In the movie *Shrek*, Fiona is a princess who is ugly but nice. Create another ugly but nice princess and write a description of her—without using the words *ugly* or *nice*. (You may want to consult a thesaurus for help.)

47.
Complete this sentence 15 different ways:

If only... then...

48.
Make up the perfect friend for yourself.
What is this person like? Be as specific as possible.

49. Do you have a responsibility to others? If so, to whom? Why? If not, why not? Explain.

50. Some people can turn anything into a drama. They drop their toast, jelly side down. Tragedy! What will they ever do? How can they go on living?

Describe a small, inconsequential annoyance, from the point of view of a drama king or queen.

51. What kind of sleeper are you? Are you a light sleeper? A heavy sleeper? Do you wake up easily? Do you ignore the alarm? Do you snore? Do you sleep on your stomach? Do you wear socks? Describe your sleep habits.

52. It's interesting to watch a hockey game and see the referees simply stand to the side when a fight breaks out. They don't interfere until someone hits the ground.

Do you ever wonder if it might be a good idea to let angry people go ahead and fight it out? Or is violence nearly always a bad idea? What are your thoughts on the subject of fighting?

53.

Sometimes an author creates a character, but the character doesn't ring true. Here's an example:

Clyde was heartbroken when the love of his life, the raven-haired Ramona with the voice of an angel, left him for a computer geek from the Silicon Valley. He thought, "What does this guy have that I don't have? He writes code all day, sitting at a computer. He may have strong fingers from tapping on the computer all day, but I've got strong arms from delivering refrigerators day in and day out."

He sat in the back of his pick-up truck staring off into the night. "Dang," he thought. "I miss that little darlin' of mine. I miss the way she can wring the emotion out of an opera aria and make audiences weep with the pathos in her voice. I love the sincerity of her tone when she commands the stage. I love the way she can fry up an egg over-easy, with just the right amount of yolk left runny when she flips it onto my plate. I love the little wobbly flaps at the bottom of her ears. I just ain't gonna be the same without her."

He sighed and took a sip of his Perrier. "I fear my heart is broke. I fear I shall never recover. What will I do now? Oh, woe is me."

The paragraphs above create a rather confusing and unbelievable picture of Clyde. Rewrite, choosing details carefully to make Clyde seem more believable and real.

54. **Here's a real flexibility stretch for your brain:** Explain why the elimination of all traffic laws would be a great idea.

Imagine no stop signs, no stoplights, and no speed limits. People can drive on either side of the road. Pedestrians do not have the right of way. There *is* no right of way. No one needs to pass a driving test to drive. People of any age or any ability can drive.

Never mind what you *really* think. Give reasons why this terrible idea should be adopted, using your most convincing language.

**55.
What really made you angry recently?**
Describe what happened, vividly, but use no more than 200 words.

56. **Think back to what might be your earliest memory.** What do you remember? Try to recall as many details as possible. Where were you? Who was there? What was happening? How did you feel?

Describe the memory. Then ask yourself, "Why do I remember that?" Explore possibilities.

57. **Write a "combined" commercial** for two different products. For example, you might write a commercial that advertises both Head and Shoulders shampoo and Count Chocula cereal, or Nike running shoes and Bic pens.

58. **What has been a hard lesson for you to learn?** Explain.

59. **Someone might say, "That would be good,"** and mean, in all sincerity, that it really would be good. Another person might say, "That would be good," in a sarcastic way, meaning that it would most certainly *not* be good. Still another person might say, "That would be good," in a hesitant way, meaning, "Well, it could be good, but it might not be good, and I'm just not sure..."

Write a conversation that includes "That would be good" used in at least three ways.

60.
Write new words to
"My Bonnie Lies Over the Ocean."
Your new version can't include an ocean
or a sea or even a Bonnie.
Here are the original words:

My Bonnie lies over the ocean.
My Bonnie lies over the sea.
My Bonnie lies over the ocean.
Oh, bring back my Bonnie to me.

Bring back, bring back,
Oh, bring back my Bonnie to me, to me.
Bring back, bring back.
Oh, bring back my bonnie to me.

61. **How do you doodle?** Some experts believe that we all doodle in the same basic patterns and that people throughout history have also doodled in the same basic patterns. Looking at your own doodling patterns, do you think this could be true? Do you think the shaded cube you drew during the last boring meeting was also drawn by a cave man long ago? Consider the doodling of others you know, too.

On a related note, why do you think people doodle? Do you believe that doodling reveals anything about a person? If so, what?

62. **Nearly everyone has a television show, a book, or a movie** that they are a little embarrassed about liking—a guilty pleasure. Do you? What is it? Why do you like it? Why are you a little embarrassed about liking it? Who would you *not* want to know that you like it? Explain.

63. **Describe one small act of courage that you admire.** Perhaps it's something you witnessed. Perhaps it's something you heard or read about. Perhaps it's something you experienced. Perhaps it's something you did yourself, to your surprise. Whatever it is, describe it.

Remember, it's a small act. A small act of courage is *not* facing down an angry mob all alone or rushing into a burning building and saving six children. Those are big acts. A small act is one that perhaps doesn't make a big difference in the world but *does* make a real difference to someone somewhere, somehow, in some memorable way.

64. Describe a change you have loved.

65. Describe a change you have hated.

66. **Stretch your mind.** What do canned peas and an accordion have in common? What does a bathroom faucet have in common with an algebra book? What does the windshield on a bus have in common with a goldfish? Think outside the box to find similarities. Explain them.

67.
Trenton Trilby has written a book. Write a description of the book for the book jacket, using the letters "tr" as many times as possible.

---

68. **Think of someone you dislike a lot.** Give the person a pseudonym. Then write down ten qualities, characteristics, or actions you don't like about the person. Be as specific as possible.

69. **There is a theory that what we dislike most in others** is related to something we don't like about ourselves. What connection can you find between the list you made and what you dislike in yourself? Examine the connections. Is there truth to the theory? Explain.

70. **Reach for the stars. She wanted the moon. He thinks he's the center of the universe.** How many everyday sentences can you write that use *star, moon, universe,* or some other term from our solar system?

Use sentences that people are likely to hear or read. "I think I'll mosey on over to the moon" is a sentence a person is unlikely to hear, ever. "It was a star-studded program" is something a person might easily hear or read on any given day.

71.
What do you have faith in?
Is it love? Kindness? God? Democracy? Truth? Justice? Karma? Family? Or...? Explain.

72.

Little John looked up at the uncle he was meeting for the first time and said, matter-of-factly, "You sure are fat."

"How come your nose is so big?" another child asked of a perfect stranger.

Another child decided, out of the blue, to share with the people in the supermarket the fact that her daddy took money out of her piggy bank for beer (He had, because he didn't have any cash, but he put it right back the next day.)

What if people never learned to keep their thoughts and questions to themselves? Create a character who lives in such a world. Write a description of the character's visit to the supermarket, or Miss Elpsbah's house, or the principal's office, or some other place of your choice. What and who does your character encounter? What does your character say? What do others say? Describe the scene.

73. **Verbs, verbs, verbs.** They make writing interesting. Good old Joe can *walk* into the room, but that's a bit *pedestrian* (a little writer's joke there!). How much more interesting it is if he *limps* or *strolls* or *toddles* or *ambles* into the room.

Imagine someone named Natalie. She *sits*. She *looks* at someone. Choosing verbs carefully, create a much more vivid and precise picture of what Natalie is doing.

> **74. You've got an idea for a new Olympic event,** unlike anything that has been seen in past Olympic games. Make your pitch to the Olympic committee, in 100 words or less.

75. **Describe one moment in time** that had some significance for you. What happened? Was it something unusual? Funny? Tragic? Momentous? Thrilling? Was it just an ordinary moment that somehow caused you to appreciate something? Was it a memorable event that changed your life forever? Describe the moment and explain its significance.

76. **Describe, in detail, a tiny defect**—a scab on your elbow, a loose button, a chip on your tooth, a pimple on your nose, a pimple on someone else's nose, a rattle in the car door, a scuff on your shoe, a dent in a can of corn, a knob on the television, a stuck zipper, a hangnail, a crack in a cup, a scratch on your sunglasses, a tear in the page of a book, a broken hook on an earring, or...? Tell the world more than it ever wanted to know about this tiny defect.

> **77. How many ways can you find to say "She is smart"**—without actually saying "She is smart"?

78. Some parents are paralyzed when naming their children,
thinking of all of the potentially awful nicknames other kids might come up with, from either the name itself or the child's initials. The truth is that kids can make a joke out of nearly any name, if they want.

Describe your experiences with nicknames. Has anyone ever made fun of your name? If so, how? Have you ever been the one to twist other kids' names in cruel or amusing ways? Are nicknames sometimes forms of endearment?

79. In Robert Frost's poem "Fire and Ice," he ponders whether the world will end in fire or ice. How do you think the world will end—ice age, global warming, Biblical apocalypse, or...? Explain.

80. How did you find out there is no Santa Claus,
or no tooth fairy, or no Easter bunny? Describe what happened and how you felt.

81. Which of these "p" words
best describes you:
perky, practical, patient, portly, productive, powerful, playful, pragmatic, purposeful, or *pessimistic?* Explain.

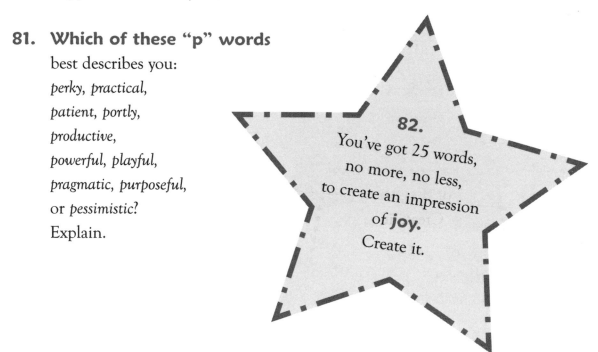

82.
You've got 25 words, no more, no less, to create an impression of **joy.**
Create it.

83. A Colorado restaurant has a sign that reads, "Misbehaving children will be sold as slaves." A Chicago coffee shop has incited controversy with a sign reading, "Children of all ages must behave and use their indoor voices." Another store has a sign that reads, "Misbehaving children will be given a cup of espresso and a puppy." Are you offended by such signs? Why? Do you applaud them? Why? What are your thoughts about children's behavior in public places?

84. You've got 25 words, no more, no less, to create an impression of **sadness**. Create it.

85. You've got 25 words, no more, no less, to create an impression of **disgust**. Create it.

86. List your top five favorite movies of all time. What do these choices say about who you are? Explain.

87. **Robert Fulghum's book,** *All I Really Need to Know I Learned in Kindergarten,* includes such advice as, "Share everything," "Clean up your own mess," and "flush." The book has been so popular it has generated many spin-off advice books—*All I Really Need to Know I Learned from Watching Star Trek, All I Need to Know I Learned from My Cat, Everything I Need to Know I Learned from Other Women, Everything I Know About Business I Learned from Monopoly,* etc.

    Write your own "All I Really Need to Know" list. First choose a place, person, or other subject you have learned from. Then create a list of what you learned from it.

88.
Write five sentences with music puns. Examples:

- *Accordion* to witnesses, she was wearing a tight *polka-*dotted dress when she *waltzed* in as though she owned the place.
- *Violins* followed when two men began arguing over her.

---

89. **Someone who has been asleep since 1952** suddenly wakes up and plops into your life. She is puzzled by a lot, but one thing that particularly puzzles her is the *www.somethingorother* she sees at the end of every advertisement.

    "They are web sites," you explain.

    "What is a web site?" she asks.

    Explain. (Good luck. Remember, this person fell asleep before computers were even around, at least for ordinary people.)

90. If you are an adult with children, describe one thing you would do differently about raising your kids, if you could start over.

If you don't have kids, or if you are still a kid yourself, tell what you will be sure *never* to do if you do have children. Be sure to explain your reasoning.

91. What has been a hard lesson for you to learn? Explain.

92. Describe five ways you are like the current president of the United States.

93. Describe five ways you are unlike the current president of the United States.

94. What characteristics do you have that would make you a good president of the United States, if only you could be elected? What qualities would hurt you in the presidency?

95. Write a fairy tale that begins with "Everyone lived happily ever after," and ends with "Once upon a time."

96.

Authors tell us something about characters through both carefully chosen details and the language their characters use. Imagine the different impressions the details and dialogue help create in these sentences:

"I don't know nothing about that, and I ain't saying nothing," said the woman, slamming her Budweiser down on the tray of the baby's high chair.

"I'm so frightfully sorry," said the woman, setting her champagne glass down carefully on the grand piano, "but I'm afraid I can contribute nothing."

Imagine two very different characters. Put them both in the position of being confronted by an authority figure. Use dialogue and details to tell us something about each character, using no more than two sentences each.

97. **For nearly everyone, songs trigger memories.** For one person, hearing a certain song reminds her of dancing with her first boyfriend. Another song makes her cry because it was the song sung at her grandfather's funeral. Another song makes her think of an absolutely insignificant moment several years ago when she was eating a stalk of asparagus and the song was playing on the radio.

What song triggers a memory for you? What do you remember? Why do you think you remember it?

98.
What makes you cry: the news, TV shows, nothing, stories about children getting hurt, or...? Why?

If you don't cry, what would make you cry, if you *did* cry?

99. **How many ways can you find to say "I hate that!"** without actually saying "I hate that!"?

100. **What happened before Goldilocks got to the bears' house?** Why was she out walking in the woods, anyway? Where were her parents? Or the babysitter? What were bears doing in a house? Tell the story.

101. **Describe a strange or unexplained incident in your life.** It doesn't have to be a big one (though it could be), like witnessing what looked like a UFO landing in your backyard. Has something you own oddly disappeared? Has someone ever known something about you that was seemingly impossible for him to know? Have you ever known something was going to happen before it did? Have you ever experienced a strange coincidence? Explain.

102. **Here are the characters in a new play:**

Super Computer Man
Aunt Bee
Gilligan
Marcia Brady

Write the beginning of the play. (If some of these characters seem familiar to you from television, you may use their television personalities for the play, if you like. If you aren't familiar with the television characters, feel free to create your own personalities for them.)

103. **"They are nice people."**

"He's a *nice* boy."
"Here's a *nice* piece of fish."
"That was *nice* of you."

Nice clearly has a broad range of meanings. Discuss what nice really means, in a nice little paragraph of nicely written sentences.

104.
When have you stuck your foot in your mouth? What happened? What did you do to try to correct the problem—or did you? How did others react to what you said? Explain.

105.
What bumper sticker sums up one of your viewpoints? Expand on the bumper sticker. Why is it right, as far as you're concerned?

106.
What have you ever
fallen in love with,
other than a person?
Explain.

107. **Describe yourself, being absolutely factual,** in one paragraph. Do not throw in any opinion.

108. **Describe yourself as your greatest fans might write about you on your best day**—you hope. Use only one paragraph.

109. **Write about a memory that involves a car.** Have you ever been embarrassed by a car you or someone else was driving? Did you ever get sick in a car as a child? Were you ever bored to death on a car trip? Have you ever been envious of someone's car? Have you ever had an adventure in a car? Pull up a car memory and describe it.

110. **It is commonly believed that the longer people are married** the more they begin to look alike. Do you think this is true? Why or why not?

113. Complete this sentence 10 different ways:

Fear is...

111.
What is the worst advice you have ever heard—or given? Why was it so bad? Explain.

112.
What is the best advice you have ever heard—or given? Why was it so good? Explain.

114. **"I have observed that people who talk on cell phones** are way more likely than other phone talkers to end conversations with, 'I love you,'" said Howard. "I once sat on a plane beside two women who called at least seven people each and ended each call with 'I love you.'"

If Howard is correct in his observation (and never mind whether or not you personally agree that it's true), what might account for the more frequent use of "I love you" to end cell phone calls? Come up with some plausible explanations and describe them.

115. **Does your stomach talk to you?** Does it flip-flop when you are nervous? Does it burn when you are worried? Does it completely forget about food when you are stressed out? Write about how your stomach mirrors your mood.

If your stomach doesn't talk to you, which part of your body does reflect your emotions? Is it your head? Your back? Or...? Explain.

116. **Are you a morning person or a night person?** An introvert or an extrovert? Do you see the glass as half empty or half full? Discuss.

117. **Write about a *first* in your life:** first date, first funeral, first communion, first car, first time you drove a car, first time you stayed home alone, etc. Choose one first and write about the experience. What happened? How did you feel? How did the experience work out?

118. **Jeremy's class assignment was to write about a happy event in his life.** Here is the first paragraph of the paper he turned in:

I liked it a lot when my sister got in trouble for the mess and not me. It was great. I was so happy I could hardly stand it.

Jeremy's teacher looks at the paper, hands it back, and says, "Elaborate." Help Jeremy out by rewriting the paragraph, with details.

119. **Describe a small improvement that you appreciate** in your life, even if that improvement has been around for quite a while.

Heather, for example, appreciates her feather pillow every single night, even though it's several years old. She remembers the thick foam pillow she had before, which made her neck hurt. She is still surprised to scrunch up the feather pillow and find that it stays just the way she wants it to under her neck, instead of popping back into a firm rectangle.

What do you appreciate?

120.

If you had to choose one of the following to run our country, would you choose **big government, big business, or Big Bird?**

Why? Explain.

121.
Look at the sea of words below:

connections   Iraq   puppies   saxophone
fury   Mount Everest   daylight saving time
SUV   cable television   disappointment
dump trucks   bib   diamond   dumpling
confusion   airport   rugby   cactus   silent
nursing home   moon   orange   knitting
quarter   potential   text messaging   anime
Snickers   alligator   licorice   gentle
watermelon   awkward   surf   Slinky   hip-hop
Microsoft   balloon   loud   rude
misbehave   clothesline   drums   brother   airbag

Which words make you feel a prickle of interest? (It may not be a *big* prickle.) Which ones stand out the most, perhaps calling to mind a scene, an emotion, an anecdote, an experience?

Pick one of the words that, for whatever reason, seems most interesting to you. Explore in writing what comes to mind, in any form you like—poetry, prose, essay, play, letter, etc.

122. **Who can explain the enduring popularity of the "Itsy Bitsy Spider" song?** It's simple, but it's not exactly exciting.

A spider climbs up a water spout. The rain washes him down. He climbs back up the spout again. Only very young children are likely to find this interesting at all, and that's probably because of the hand motions.

Write lyrics for a spider song likely to appeal to older children, or even adults. (For a more intensive brain stretch, write the music, too!)

123. **"He's so tall he could hunt ducks with a rake."**

"He's so short he has to stand on a stool to reach his socks."

"He's so mean, he scares himself whenever he walks into the room."

Write five more "He's so..." or "She's so..." sentences. Try for both exaggeration and originality.

124.
What are you missing?
Interpret the question in whatever way seems relevant to you.

125. **A person's big talents are usually obvious**—being a riveting speaker, a gifted pianist, an award-winning painter. Whatever your big talents are, ignore them for a moment. What are your *small* talents?

   Maybe you can tell whether or not items of clothing will fit you or someone else, by just looking at them. Maybe you can make an absolutely perfect bowl of popcorn, the old fashioned way. Maybe you can take the smallest incident and retell it so that people think it is funny. Whatever small talents you may have, describe them. Don't be modest!

126.
Here is your character: Pat.

Who is Pat? You decide. Create him or her, imagining many details about the character. For example, does Pat like vegetables? What disappoints Pat? What recently made Pat happy? How happy? What does Pat like to do on Sunday afternoons? Think about Pat until he or she is clear in your mind.

   Then, using what you know about your character, describe Pat's meeting with someone else, about something, somewhere.

127. **What kind of music are you?** Are you salsa or rap? Classical or reggae? Rock and roll or new age? Or...? Explain.

128. **"Life is a thump-ripe melon—so sweet and such a mess,"** according to musician Greg Brown in one of his songs. What else is life, besides a thump-ripe melon?

Compare life to a food, following the form of Brown's line: "Life is a _____ — _____."

129. **What do you dislike that no one else** (or hardly anyone else) seems to dislike? Why do you dislike it? Why do you think you are pretty much alone in your feelings? Explain.

130.
Write a teeny-tiny,
two-line poem
with a long, long title.
Example:

What Jamal Had On His Hands the Morning
After He Accidentally Gave his Puppy Exedrin PM
instead of the Anti-Worm Medication

Groggy
doggie.

131. **Write a paragraph that uses all these words:** *dabble, gobble, hobble, bobble, wobble.*

132.

What do you do, over and over again, that's really pretty silly?

Do you open the refrigerator, looking for something good to eat, find nothing that appeals to you, and come back ten minutes later to look again, kind of hoping that maybe something good has materialized since your last look?

Do you refuse to throw away that shirt you've been meaning to iron for the last three years, even though you never wear it and you know, deep down, that you never will actually iron it?

Do you cut teeny slices from the pan of brownies instead of taking a whole piece, thinking that the calories in the little pieces don't really count?

Describe something silly you do, again and again.

133. Characters in movies are different from people in real life. Movie people who go grocery shopping always come home with a baguette sticking out of their grocery bag, which is always brown paper. Real people usually buy loaves of bread instead of baguettes, but when they do buy a baguette, they often bring it home in a plastic bag.

**134.
Are you an early, late, or on-time person?**
Why? What do you think made you that way? How do you feel about being that way? How do others feel about it? Explain.

Movie people often hurry into their homes and forget to close the door, even when they live in a dangerous area or know that some evil creature is stalking them. Real people usually close their doors behind them. Movie people walk into other people's homes without knocking, so they can discover something surprising. Real people knock.

Think of other ways that movie people are different from real people. Describe the differences.

135.
Write a story that includes all of the following words:

galaxy, supermodel, coffee, tunnel, scarf, antlers.

136. What small invention has made a big difference in your life? Is it fake nails, TiVo, Netflix, a treadmill, washable markers and crayons, electric-heated mattress pad, or...? Explain.

137. **Comedians and many others** over the years have contended that some words are just naturally funnier than others. Some, for example, believe that *duck* is the funniest word. Cartoonist Gary Larson has said that *cow* is just naturally funny. Comedian George Carlin has said that naturally funny words include *kumquat, succotash,* and *guacamole.* A character in Neil Simon's play, *The Sunshine Boys*, states that words with "k" in them are funny (*pickle, chicken*), while words with "l" and "m" are not.

  What do you think? What words are funny to you? Do you have any idea why? Explain.

**138.
If you were a computer**, would you be a Mac or a PC? A laptop or a desktop? Explain.

139. **A four-year-old girl once declared: "When I'm a mommy,** I'm going to tell my kids how many pounds I am." Should people be honest and open about their weight? Or is their weight nobody else's business? Why do so many people fudge their weight for driver licenses and other documents, even though it doesn't change anything? Why are people so sensitive about discussing weight?

140. **Should people report others for minor crimes**, such as littering, violation of noise ordinances or not following lawn-watering restrictions? Why or why not? Explain.

141. **What is something you really, really wanted** and never got? How did you cope? Did you suffer as a result? How would your life be different if you had gotten what you wanted? Explain.

142. **Everyone has a role in his or her family.** Are you the family clown? The black sheep? The good student? The athlete? The caretaker? The crazy maker? What is your role in your family? How do you feel about this role?

143. **Have you ever heard the wrong words** in a song? When Elton John sings: "Hold me closer, tiny dancer," some have thought they were hearing, "Hold me close, like Tony Danza." Others have the heard ABBA's lyrics, "Dancing queen/Feel the beat from the tambourine," as "Dancing queen/Steve McQueen on the tambourine."

Write about lyrics that you have misheard. What did you hear? What are the correct lyrics? Does your version of the lyrics make sense? How did you learn that what you heard was wrong?

**144.
Of all these "e" words, which one best describes you:**

*empathetic,
energetic,
elusive,
extroverted,
egalitarian,
ethical,* or
earthy?

Why? Explain.

145. **Describe your ultimate road trip.** Who would you bring? Where would you go? What would you pack? What would you drive? How long would you be gone?

146. **Many people secretly** (or not so secretly) take an interest in at least one tabloid story every year—perhaps a story about a political embarrassment, a high-profile romance, or a celebrity marriage, break-up, or pregnancy. Which tabloid news story has held your interest recently? Why?

147. **Write about a trip to the grocery store.** Is it a surreal late night trip to buy ice cream? Is it an annoying trip with kids in tow? Is it a junk food fest? Is it a shopping trip where you seek out the only the healthiest food, like flax seed or organic yogurt? Include details of your feelings, your surroundings, your thoughts and what ends up in your shopping cart.

148. **Write a story or anecdote that starts with** "I hated my dumpy-looking shadow" and ends with "That's never going to happen."

149. **What makes you smile every time you think of it?** Do you smile because it's funny, because it's sweet, or for some other reason?

150.
"I was speechless."
"Words can't begin to describe how I felt."
"I was at a loss for words."

When have you been unable to find the right words to express what you wanted to express? Describe the circumstances. What happened? Who was involved? How did you feel?

151.

People are always saying, "There are only two kinds of people in the world." What would you add to the following list?

There are only two kinds of people in the world:

- those who recycle and those who still throw trash out their car windows.
- those who who pay attention to the news and those who have a hard time remembering who the president is.
- those who can understand why someone would become a vegan, and those who think not eating meat is grounds for seeking psychiatric help.

152. What really annoys you? Is it paying over $4.00 for water at the movie theater, people who don't vote but have plenty to say about politics, tattling children, people who don't respond to e-mail, people who say, "Not to be mean, but..." and then go on to be mean? Write about what gets under your skin. Feel free to use strong (though not off-color or offensive) language.

153. Bill Maher's show on HBO lists his "New Rules" each week. With them, he tells how the world would run if he were making the rules. What would your "new rules for the world" be? Examples:

- New rule: Magazines can't have all those little inserts in them that fall out when you open the magazine.
- New rule: People over 40 can't say "Dude!" or "Whassup!"
- New rule: Clerks at the cash register in a store can't take phone calls while paying customers wait.

154. Which of these "r" words best describes you: radical, raucous, realistic, radiant, revolutionary, regretful, run of the mill, refined or rock solid? Explain.

155. The ancient Greeks believed that hospitality was one of the greatest virtues, and *hubris* (overbearing pride or arrogance) was one of the greatest character flaws. Does this philosophy make sense to you? If not, why not? In your opinion, what is the greatest virtue? What is the greatest character flaw?

156. Describe your favorite color from the point of view of each of your five senses. For example, black might taste like licorice. Gray might smell like rain. Pink might feel like bubblegum.

158. Oxygen bars, 24-hour news, iPods, belly button rings... Choose one thing from our current age that your great-great-grandparents would have a hard time understanding. How would you explain it?

157. What small pleasure would you never want to live without? Is it Indian food, your favorite Dixie Chicks CD, e-mail, Elizabeth George mysteries, decaf lattés, your cell phone, or...? Explain.

159. How are you too hard on yourself? Or are you? Explain.

160. You have just finished writing your autobiography, which includes 10 different chapters. Write the title of each chapter in the book.

161. Imagine that you could take one small step tomorrow to improve your life. What are some of the small steps you might consider? Why? Is there any reason you don't take these steps?

162. If you wanted to write under a pen name, what might yours be? Why?

163. **Write about a toy** you remember well from childhood. Why did you like it? Where did you get it? Did it belong to you or someone else? Was it a gift from someone special? Why do you think you remember it? Did you play with it alone or with someone else? Do you still have it? If not, do you know where it is now? Explain.

164. **In Greek mythology, Cassandra could predict bad things** before they happened, though no one would believe her. Have you ever felt like Cassandra? When? If not, would you ever want to? What would be the advantages? The disadvantages? Explain.

165. **When did you first realize that your parents did NOT know everything?** Explain.

166. **Write a conversation between a modern person** and a person or character from the past.

    Examples: Jennifer Aniston and Ophelia. George W. Bush and Thomas Jefferson. John Elway and Odysseus. Britney Spears and Queen Elizabeth.

167. **What makes your skin crawl?** Explain.

168. **What makes your hair stand on end?** Explain.

169. **What makes your heart ache?** Explain.

170. **What makes your stomach turn?** Explain.

171. **What makes your head hurt?** Explain.

172. **What makes your knees weak?** Explain.

173. Many people have cell phones, but even more people have *opinions* about cell phones. Choose a topic related to cell phones, and write about your views. Here are a few possible ideas for exploration:

- Do you have a cell phone? If not, do you wish you had one, or are you proud to be cell phone free? Do you feel under-connected? Or do you believe that a cell phone would make you over-connected?

- The comedian George Carlin, in one of his stand-up routines, wonders if Bach ever intended for any of his beautifully composed music to become downloadable as a cell-phone ring. What do you think about cell-phone rings? Do you think they are annoying? Amusing? Silly? Or...?

- How do you feel about people talking on a cell phone while driving?

- Do you ever see people walking down the street but not interacting with one another because one or more of them is talking on a cell phone? Do you think there is something weird about that? Why or why not?

- Should cell phones be checked in before people enter theaters?

- How do you feel about overhearing very personal cell phone conversations?

174. Do you believe there is such a thing as love at first sight? Why or why not? Explain.

175. If you could have a robot that did all of the chores that you loathe, what would you have the robot do? Why?

176.

People are complicated. They all have personality traits and beliefs that define who they are. Sometimes, however, these traits and/or beliefs clash, creating a contradiction.

For example, a person might be an animal-rights activist who eats meat. She might be a health nut who smokes cigarettes or a feminist leader who buys her daughter Barbie dolls. He might be a person who believes in *truth* as a guiding principle of his life, but who lies to his children about all the trouble he got into when he was a teenager.

Think about a contradiction that is part of who you are. Why do you think you developed these conflicting traits or beliefs? Have you ever struggled between the conflicting parts of your personality? Do they bother you, or have you accepted them? How do others react? Explain.

177.

If you could, what would you put in a time capsule, so it would always stay the same?

Would it be the haircut you got two weeks ago, when it looked perfect for one day? Would it be your little nephew's funny way of saying "got-for" instead of "forgot"? Would it be the five minutes after you have accomplished something and feel good about it, before you begin to worry about your next project?

Write about something you would bottle up and save forever.

178. What sometimes disappoints you about someone? Are your expectations reasonable? Explain.

179. A prankster once sent a letter to "Dear Abby" that was based on an episode of *The Simpsons* television show. While merely fiction, the letter was believable enough that Abby actually answered it in one of her columns.

Write your own really believable, though prank, "Dear Abby" letter, asking for her advice. (Don't send it though. The columnist has more than enough real problems to address.)

180. What's in a name? In the past, a woman in the United States always took her husband's name when she married. In fact, she had to, as a matter of law.

Now, however, many women keep their names when they marry. Some married couples even make up entirely new last names for themselves.

Do you think naming "rules" are important? Do names matter at all? What do you think is most important to remember about names?

181. Start a story with, "You are nothing to me but a smear on the sports page of the morning paper." End the story with, "Don't you want dessert?"

182. Write a story that begins and ends with the word *average*.

183.

What do you kind-of-sort-of feel to be true, though you know it makes no logical sense? Do you kind-of-sort-of believe that you really go someplace in your dreams? Do you kind-of-sort-of believe that you might once have visited a parallel universe? Do you kind-of-sort-of believe that computers and cars can sometimes heal themselves, if you ignore a problem long enough? Describe one of your kind-of-sort-of-beliefs.

184. Who has the easier life, boys or girls? Men or women? Explain.

185. Who do you think has the more interesting life, boys or girls? Men or women? Explain.

186. What do you think males secretly—or not so secretly—envy about females? What do you think females secretly—or not so secretly—envy about males? (Remember, you are not necessarily writing about *your* beliefs.)

187. Write a YES story—a paragraph where the first sentence starts with the letter "y," the second with "e," the third with "s." Repeat the pattern until you have finished the paragraph. And, yes, the last sentence must begin with the letter "s."

188.
Write about a lie.
Was it your lie? Was it someone else's lie? What were the consequences of the lie? Were they positive? Negative? What feelings were involved?

189.
Choose an object in your house.
List five words that would best describe the object. Then write a description of the object *without* using those five words.

190.
Watch yourself, as if you were a dog.
As the dog observes you, what does it see? What does it think? How does it comment to itself? Write out the dog's observations about you.

191. **What tradition means a lot to you?** Why? Is it a holiday tradition, like cutting your own Christmas tree? Is it running four miles in the prairie every morning with your friend, followed by a cup of home-brewed Starbucks and the local paper? Is it giving your brother the stupidest hat you can find every year for his birthday? What silly or serious tradition has special meaning for you? Explain.

192. **Write a news story** incorporating these words: *lasagna, grizzly bear, flip-flops, moon, flag, trampoline.*

193. **Imagine that you are someone famous.** Write an obnoxious tabloid story about your famous self. Make sure to include quotations from un-named sources close to you.

194. **An INXS song from the 80s** plays with words that rhyme with *mediate.* (Examples: *suffocate, alleviate, hate, mate, depreciate,* etc.) Write an article, story, or poem that includes at least 20 different words that rhyme with *mediate.*

195. **Here's your title: *Empty.*** Create a piece of writing that fits that title.

196.

Who would star in the movie of your life?
Who would you want to play you? Who do you think the studio would cast in your role? Are they the same person? Explain.

197.

Here's an Italian proverb:

**Since the house is on fire,
let us warm ourselves.**

Write a fable that ends with this proverb.

198.

Write a paragraph or story that
includes at least
**25 words that rhyme
with *free*.**

199.

Are you the oldest of your siblings? The youngest? A middle child? What are the disadvantages of being born in your birth order? If you are an only child, what are the disadvantages of being an only child? Be as specific as you can. (Feel free to be as petty as you like, too. Here's your chance to complain, if you want.)

200.

Describe one little thing you liked when you were a small child. Make it a small *like*, not a big *love*.

Did you like having Grandpa "whisker" you when he came over? Did you like making Uncle Emilio sing "I Ain't Nothin' But a Hound Dog" over and over again? Did you like going to Aunt Mary's for potato pancakes?

Did you love meeting the propane delivery man who always gave you bubblegum? Maybe you remember how he had the name "Lloyd" on his uniform pocket and how you were fascinated to see that someone could have a name that started with the same two letters. Maybe you remember how you had to stand around awkwardly before he would offer you the gum, because you were too embarrassed to ask. Maybe you remember how your mother always said, "Did you tell him thank-you?" when you came back in the house.

Write all you can remember about one fond memory of something you liked as a little kid.

201. What pet would you never even consider having? Even if you are a true animal lover, there must be some pet you wouldn't want around. Why would you never even consider having this kind of pet, even if you feel kind of guilty about the reasons, and even if the reasons make no logical sense?

   Note: Consider only relatively normal pets. A tarantula, for example, is *relatively* normal since you have probably known someone who had one. A zebra, on the other hand, would definitely be out of the normal range. You probably haven't known someone who keeps zebras for pets.

202. If you were a musical instrument, which one would you be? What kind of music would you play and why?

203. How do others see you? Write a description of yourself from a friend or family member's point of view.

204. When has intuition sent you the wrong message? Explain.

205. When did you first become aware of your gender and how you are different from the opposite sex? What were the circumstances?

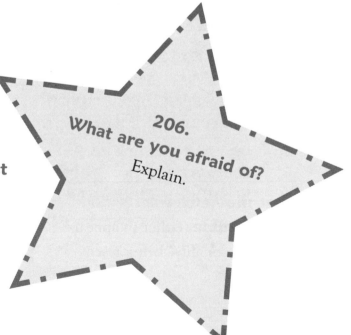

206. What are you afraid of? Explain.

207. Think about something you did in the last year that had an impact on at least one other person. What did you do? Who did it impact? Why? Was it a positive or a negative impact? Was it a big impact or a little one? Were you surprised by the impact? Explain.

208. Which one of the following words "speaks" to you?

pickles, devastation, sneezing, grandma, embarrassment, mascara, quarterback, semitruck, whales, Alka-Seltzer, Winnie the Pooh, aftershave lotion.

Choose one that stands out to you, for whatever reason. Then use that word as the starting point for a paragraph.

209. What movie character do you resemble, either in appearance or personality? Is it a resemblance you feel yourself? Is it a resemblance others see? Explain.

210.
What do you really care about? Explain.

211.
What do you really care about that is not human? Explain.

212.
What do you really care about that is not visible? Explain.

213.
What do you really care about that others don't care much about? Explain.

214.
What are you embarrassed to admit you care about? Explain.

215.

Choose a headline from a newspaper.

(It can be a regular newspaper or an online edition.) Now imagine that the headline somehow connects to your life. Write the newspaper article that shows the connection. (Yes, this may take some real stretching on your part.)

216.

Wicked, **which is both a book and Broadway musical,** tells what happens before Dorothy meets the good witch and the wicked witch in *The Wizard of Oz.*

Choose another well-known family or children's movie, such as *E.T., The Sound of Music, Shrek, Toy Story,* or *Monsters, Inc.* Choose one of the characters and explain what happens before the movie opens.

For example, you might tell how E.T. winds up in a backyard on earth. Or you might tell the story of how Maria winds up in training to be a nun. Set the stage for the real movie to open by giving us some background.

217. Think of a person who really makes an impression of some kind, positive or negative. Is it a political figure? A musician? An actor? A neighbor? A teacher? A child? A checker at the supermarket? Whoever it is, what kind of impression does that person make? Does the person portray an overall image of strength? Leadership? Kindness? Charisma? Charm? Joyousness? Pessimism? Or...?

Think about the impression the person makes, and then write a description that conveys that impression. In other words, show the person in action, making an impression.

For example, you might describe a senator talking to a group of citizens and inspiring them to take an action of some kind. You might describe your neighbor shoveling an elderly couple's walk, creating an impression of quiet kindness and thoughtfulness. You might describe a little girl batting her eyes at her daddy and creating an impression of manipulative power.

218. "What goes around comes around" is what people sometimes say when someone wrongs them and gets away with it. Do you believe it is true? Do you believe that people someday pay for their crimes, whether or not they go unpunished at the time? Explain your views.

219.

Here's the scenario: A fussy eater refuses to eat the anchovy and goat cheese salad. The salad maker smacks him or her with a spatula. Everyone laughs.

Write a paragraph about this incident, adding details to make it make sense. Make readers sympathize much more with one of the characters than the others.

220.

Think about a room or specific place you remember well from when you were a young child. Maybe it was your bedroom, the basement playroom, the backyard, your friend's kitchen, or the principal's office. (You don't have to remember it in a *good* way!) Draw a floor plan of the room or place. Where was each item in the room? Were there windows? Where were the doors, plants, closets?

As you draw the floor plan, what memories come to you? Does drawing the desk in the corner remind you of sitting there the time your friend accidentally jammed your hand with a pencil, leaving a pencil lead mark in your palm that is still there to this day? Does drawing the white chair in the living room remind you of your mother's admonition never to sit in that chair—and how you did anyway once when she was gone and dropped chocolate syrup on it?

Choose one memory that surprises you. Write about it. What did you remember? Why does it surprise you? Is it a pleasant memory? An unpleasant memory? Explain.

221.

You are a computer geek. Write a love letter to the geek of your dreams.

222.

You are a politician. Write a love letter to the politician of your dreams.

223.

You are a hot celebrity. Write a love letter to the hot celebrity of your dreams.

224.

You are a poet. Write a love letter to the poet of your dreams.

225. Alphabet books often have a theme of some kind. Just a handful of the titles currently available are *The Farm Alphabet Book*, *The Underwater Alphabet Book*, *The Icky Bug Alphabet Book*, *My Spiritual Alphabet Book*, *M is for Music: a Music Alphabet Book*, *O is for Orca: a Pacific Northwest Alphabet Book*, and *The Desert Alphabet Book*.

Writers interested in writing an alphabet book on a theme are usually advised to start with the hard letters. If they can't come up with a solution for "Q" or "Z" or "K," they probably need to change themes.

Try your hand at writing an alphabet book, on a theme not for little kids. (That doesn't mean it's X-rated—just not for little kids.) For example, you might try "cool cars" or "great books" or "what every home needs." Write the entries for the hard letters first, to make sure your theme is do-able.

226. People often think of great comebacks or eloquent arguments long after they need them. Have you ever thought of just the right thing to say in a tense situation, long after the situation has passed? Write about a particularly frustrating moment and all the things you *might* have said, if only you had thought of them at the time.

227. Have you ever had an awful time doing something everyone else thought was a lot of fun? Have you ever had a wonderful time doing something others hated? Have you ever expected to enjoy something, only to find that you hated it? Write about your experiences and how they filled, or didn't fulfill, your expectations.

228. Teachers have heard every excuse in the book—except for the one you are about to come up with. Write a note to a teacher with a unique and creative excuse for not having an assignment finished.

229.

You've got the blues, and you want to sing about them. Write a song.

Choose something specific as the subject of your song. Is it your problem understanding trigonometry? Is it the trouble you have with your boss at work? Is it the fact that you can't get enough help with the housework that needs to be done?

If you need help getting started, you might try a technique used in many blues songs—making a list of what's wrong.

Example:

My boss puts me to sleep in meetings.
He's always yelling at the staff.
He's got the personality of an aardvark.
He doesn't know how to laugh!

230.

You are a psychologist who is writing an article called "Battle for Control of the Remote Control—An Analysis of Family Behaviors and Conflicts." Write at least one paragraph of your article. What behaviors have you observed? What do you think they mean? What importance do your observations have for society? (A mock-serious tone to your writing might prove effective here!)

231. Emily Post's 1922 book, *Etiquette,* **was quite popular in its day,** selling over a million copies. Here are some examples of its advice:

- *There is no rudeness greater than for (a gentleman) to stand talking to a lady with his hat on, and a cigar or cigarette in his mouth.*
- *Whether in a private carriage, a car or a taxi, a lady must never sit on a gentleman's left; because according to European etiquette, a lady "on the left" is not a "lady."*

Clearly, times have changed. What is one area of modern life that you think could use some clear and specific rules of etiquette? Would it involve cell phones? Driving in heavy traffic? Using skateboards? Answering e-mail? Sharing lockers at school? Working out at a health club? Dealing with unruly children in restaurants? Or?

Write the etiquette rules for one specific area of modern-day life.

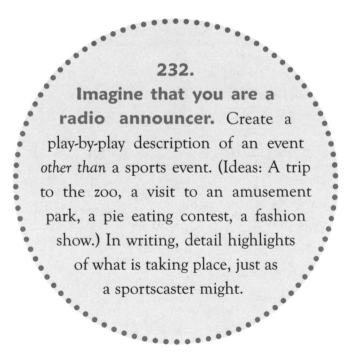

232.
Imagine that you are a radio announcer. Create a play-by-play description of an event *other than* a sports event. (Ideas: A trip to the zoo, a visit to an amusement park, a pie eating contest, a fashion show.) In writing, detail highlights of what is taking place, just as a sportscaster might.

233.
Create your own resumé, featuring your fabulous social skills, your keen intelligence, your emotional maturity, and all your other wonderful personal attributes. You have permission to make yourself sound like the most talented person born since Leonardo da Vinci. No exaggeration is too extreme for this resumé.

234.
Create a resumé about you, written by someone who has had just about enough of you. This person does not think you are the greatest thing since macaroni and cheese. This person is secretly substituting this resumé for the one you accidentally left in the photocopy machine.

235.
In the cartoon strip *Peanuts*, which character are you the most like? Why? Explain.

236. **A popular exhibit in many museums around the country is "Grossology,"** which deals with the science behind bodily functions such as urination, passing gas, sneezing, burping, etc.

Suppose you were to do your own "grossology" display about the grossology of where you spend most of each day. If you spend most of the day in school, one display might be the bottom of gym bags, or the back of lockers. If you are at home all day with a baby, it might be the grossology of decaying dirty diapers in the trash. If you work in an office, it might be the grossology of the smelly food a coworker forgets in the refrigerator for a month.

Choose three items for your exhibit, and write a paragraph for the signage that will go beside each display.

237. **Connections so often exist between the most unlikely people,** places, things, and events—if only we look below the surface. For example, a visitor to this planet might not at first see a connection between television sets and obesity. Yet, the growth of obesity in this country has been attributed, in large part, to people watching television and sitting at computers, rather than going outside to play, work, or exercise. What connections can you see between another pair of seemingly unrelated things? Explain.

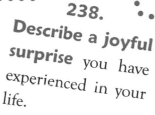

238. Describe a joyful surprise you have experienced in your life.

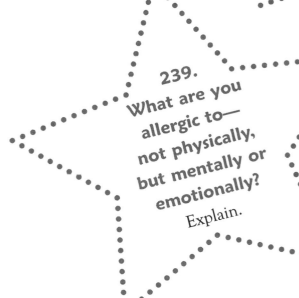

239. What are you allergic to— not physically, but mentally or emotionally? Explain.

240.

Think of a completely trivial incident. (You buy a half-gallon of milk at the supermarket, and the man behind you says, "Excuse me. You dropped something," and hands you a quarter…You go to the pencil sharpener to sharpen your pencil, and your friend says, "Hi."…You pause at a stoplight, look to your left, and the passenger in the car beside you smiles at you…)

Now write about the incident, but change it to add some kind of *conflict* to the situation. (The man behind you at the supermarket tells you that you dropped something, but then he smiles deviously, picks up your quarter, and puts it in his pocket. You are outraged…When you go to the pencil sharpener, your friend sticks out his foot and tries to trip you as he says, "Hi," and you get mad…The passenger in the car beside you smiles and then points and laughs at your car, clearly making fun of it and infuriating you.)

241. **Here's the first line of a short story:**

She's not home yet.

Using that first line, write the first paragraph of a short story, creating a mood of *fear.*

242. **Here's the first line of a short story:**

She's not home yet.

Again write the first paragraph of a short story, but this time create a mood of *celebration and delight.*

243. **Here's the first line of a short story:**

She's not home yet.

Again write the first paragraph of a short story, but this time create a mood of *anger.*

244. **Are you a rugged individualist?** Or are you someone who craves a community? Or are you somewhere in between? Explain.

245.
Kelly walks into the room. Tell us something important about Kelly by describing him or her only from the ankles down.

246. Who have been the best friends in your life? Have you had just one? Or have you had many? Have they changed over the years or remained the same? Are your best friends family or non-relatives? If you have many friends, is there a characteristic they have in common? Write about your friends.

247.
Imagine that you have to choose your husband or wife, based solely on the candidates' responses to five questions, designed by you. (Of course, there will be *lots* of candidates!) What questions are you going to ask? How will these questions help you choose a spouse?

(If you are already married, pretend you aren't. If you are far too young to even consider getting married, pretend you're older. Remember, you are s-t-r-e-t-c-h-i-n-g your brain and your imagination with this exercise.)

---

248. Write about a scar you have—physical or emotional. Where did you get it? How? How do you feel about it? Is it a proud reminder of something, or does it remind you of something you would prefer to forget? Explain.

249. If a storyteller tells a story about something that never happened, can it still be true? Explain.

250. Imagine a "life garden." Choose one plant that represents *you*. Choose other plants that represent other people and events in your life, good and bad.

   Then imagine a diagram of your garden. Where will *you* be located—on the sunny south side, or the shady north side? Will you be in the middle of the garden with other plants surrounding you, or will you be in a corner, away from other plants? Where will the "good" plants be in relation to you? Where will the "bad" plants be in relation to you?

   Now describe your garden. Tell what the different plants represent, and why.

251. Where were you and how did you feel when you first heard about the bombing of the World Trade Center, the explosion of the Space Shuttle Challenger, the shooting of President John F. Kennedy, or some other major news event of your lifetime?

> **252.**
> **Imagine an ordinary dinner, one that you eat often.** Describe each item as if it were a rare and exotic dish. Embellish as much as possible. (It's not macaroni and cheese.. It's perfectly cooked morsels of pasta, swimming in a delectable sauce created from a blend of imported cheeses and rich cream from happy cows.)

253. **You're probably tired of this question and its many variations:**

If you had to be stranded on a deserted island with something, what would it be?

Try answering this question instead:

If all of something in the world could be stranded on a deserted island, without you, what would you want it to be?

254. **Have you ever had to let go of a dream?** If so, was it a big one? A small one? Did you replace it with another dream? Have you ever let go of a dream because it came true? If all your dreams are intact, are they distant dreams, pie-in-the-sky dreams, realistic dreams, dreams that are really goals for you, or...? Explain.

255. **"Bridezilla" is a new word** that has caught on quickly in our culture. A "bridezilla," of course, is a bride-to-be who is so focused on her perfect day that she becomes a monster of sorts, making unreasonable demands on others. What is the worst "bridezilla" story you have ever heard? Or, is there some other kind of "zilla" you have encountered, such as a *mailzilla* who returns your letter because you wrote "299 Elm" instead of "299 Elm *Street*"?

256.

In the movie *Eternal Sunshine of the Spotless Mind,* Jim Carrey's and Kate Winslet's characters have their minds erased to remove any memories related to their relationship. If you could hire a firm to erase bits of your memory, what would you have them remove? Why?

257. Marianne loves Christmas and plans for it all year long. "It's such a wonderful family day," she says, "with such a spirit of giving and love in the air." Her husband's favorite holiday, however, is the Fourth of July, but not for sentimental reasons. He says, "Hey, it involves eating meat, drinking beer and lighting fireworks, without buying presents for anybody. I love it!" What is your favorite holiday? Why?

258. A person has only one chance to make a first impression. How much do you rely on first impressions? Do you think you can make a fair assessment of a person, based only on a first impression? If so, how can you tell? What are you paying attention to? Are your first instincts usually correct? Or have you learned that you shouldn't really rely on your first impressions? What experiences led you to that conclusion? Explain.

**259.
You've heard of couch potatoes.** Perhaps you live with one. Perhaps you *are* one. Describe a couch potato. Create a vivid picture.

260. Have you ever felt that you made a horrible first impression? Describe the situation and how you felt both during and after the encounter.

If you have never made a horrible first impression, perhaps you can describe your secret! Or perhaps you can describe a horrible impression someone else made on you.

261. What good, clean slang word or phrase do you particularly like? Which one do you particularly dislike? Why?

262. **May 21 is National Waitresses/Waiters Day.** March 21 is International Day for the Elimination of Racial Discrimination. October 2 is World Farm Animals Day. January 11 is International Thank-You Day. What (or who) else do you think deserves a day of its own? Why?

263. **No insult is considered an insult,** by some people, if it is accompanied by the words "bless her heart" (or "bless his heart"). Someone can say, "She's ugly as a post, bless her heart," or "He is the dumbest man alive, bless his heart," and it isn't considered mean.

Imagine that that little phrase worked everywhere, in all situations. A child could vent her anger at a parent by saying, "No, I won't do that, and you are the worst mom in the world, bless your heart." Or an employee could say to his boss, "Oh, go jump in the lake. There's no way I'm going to ever do what you tell me to do, bless your heart." What other uses can you imagine for "bless your heart"?

Or create a new little magic phrase that could take the sting out of words. What would be your phrase be? Why?

264.
What is wrong with testing?
What kind of testing?

265.
What is right about testing?
What kind of testing?

266.
Which is more important, a strong body, a strong mind, or a strong personality? (You can't say "all three." Choose only one.)

267.
Who really inspires you?
Don't write about that person. Write about someone who has inspired you in a smaller way.

268. **Do you like to dress up?** Sometimes? Never? Often? How do you feel when you are dressed up? Do you ever notice people treating you differently when you are dressed up? What does *dressed up* mean, to you? Is it ever disrespectful not to dress up? If so, when? If not, why not?

270. **What is the most controversial topic** you can think of? Do you like talking about it, or do you avoid talking about it? Do you feel strongly one way or the other about it? Why or why not? Do you talk about it only with people who feel the same as you? Do you talk about it only with people who do *not* feel the same way as you? Why do you think the topic is so controversial?

269. Write a poem, a paragraph, or a song on the subject "things that drip."

271. **"Build a bridge and get over it,"** is a response some people use when others are whining about a perceived slight, a small problem, or some other small or annoying matter. Think of something you are sick of hearing someone whine about. You might not be in a position to tell the person to "Build a bridge and get over it," but you can vent your frustration, privately, on paper. Write down exactly how you feel. (Maybe putting your thoughts down on paper will help *you* build a bridge and get over your problem of hearing about the problem!)

272. Imagine a couple (a male and a female) who disagree about something. How old is the couple? Are they married? What is the disagreement about? Is it a longstanding disagreement or a new one? Is it a big disagreement or a little one? How do the two show their disagreement?

Describe the couple and their disagreement as if you are an outsider observing. Don't take sides.

273. Now describe the same couple and their disagreement, only from the point of view of either the male or the female. Make the reader sympathize more with one person than the other.

274. Now create a conversation between the couple, showing their disagreement. Do they openly discuss whatever is wrong? Do they pretend to be talking about something else entirely, while getting little digs in? Do they enlist the support of others? Are they adult about their disagreement? Are they childish? Are they mean or nasty? Are they civilized? Or...?

**275.
What does hardly anybody
understand, except you?**

**276.
What do you have a very
hard time believing?**

277. Imagine catching just a glimpse of something that is surprising.
What do you see? Is it a customer taking a bite of an apple and putting it
back in the display? Is it a stern teacher laughing uproariously? Is it two
people kissing—two people you would never in a million years suspect of
even liking each other? Imagine three scenarios, and describe each
glimpse.

278. Expand one of the scenarios you described in #277, explaining
what led up to the surprising glimpse.

279. What is an embarrassing little truth about yourself? Do you
have trouble telling your right from your left? Did you never really learn
to tell time? Explain.

280. Most of us have heard fables, like the story of the little boy who cried "Wolf!" Write an original fable that ends with a moral, such as "Don't cry over spilled milk," or "Don't count your chickens before they hatch." Use a modern setting for your fable.

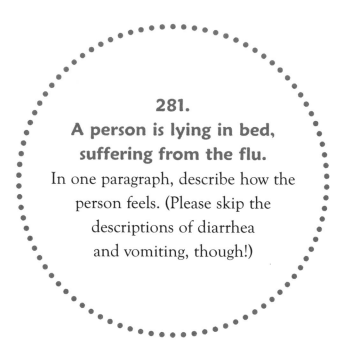

281.
A person is lying in bed, suffering from the flu.
In one paragraph, describe how the person feels. (Please skip the descriptions of diarrhea and vomiting, though!)

282. Skimble-scamble is a wonderful-sounding word. Without looking it up in the dictionary, imagine what it might mean. Write your definition and a sentence illustrating your imagined use of the word.

Then look up the word. How close was your definition? Write a new sentence using the word correctly.

283.

Think back to one of your first encounters with a baby. Who was it? Was it a sibling? A neighbor? A relative's baby? What do you remember? Why do you think you remember it?

284.

Think back to one of your first memories of an old person—or a person you thought was really old at the time. What do you remember? Why do you think you remember it?

285.

Make a list of three pairs of groups that would seem to have entirely different interests. (Examples: Monster truck fans and quilters, skateboarders and subscribers to the symphony concert series, quarterbacks and new moms.

Now choose one of the pairs and create an encounter of some kind between one or more members of each of the groups.

286.

Every few months, the toothpaste/toothbrush industry makes some amazing new "breakthrough" in the technology of tooth care—effervescent bubbles that get between the teeth, toothbrushes with extra long bristles to clean your gums, vibrating brushes, teeth whitening strips, etc.

What if all this technology could be applied to world problems instead of teeth? If you were in charge, where would you apply the technology if you could? Would you work on ways to distribute food to poor countries? Would you work on ways to lessen our country's dependence on oil? Would you find ways to reduce pollution? Or...

287.

Dan feels he sets his goals too high. When he doesn't meet them, he feels awful. He has decided he should set small and gentle goals. Then he will feel good about meeting them and be inspired to reach further goals.

Sharene, however, feels that a person should always set high goals. If she sets high goals, she will achieve a lot, even if she never reaches her goal.

Whose philosophy is correct, in your opinion? Explain.

288. Should people sing, even if they don't sing well? Should they paint, even if they don't paint well? Should they dance, even if they don't dance well? Should they play sports, even if they aren't any good? How important is the quality of what people do, versus what they might enjoy?

289.
Humans are complex.
Many of us are crushed the first time we discover someone we love or admire is not perfect. Describe a time you discovered that someone was human in a way that disappointed you.

290.
What is your attitude toward money?
Is it something to be guarded and saved? Something to be spent as soon as you get it? Something you worry about a lot? Something you are good with? Not so good with? Explain.

291.
What would you do if you won a million dollars?
Don't answer that. Instead, tell what you would definitely *not* do if you won a million dollars.

292.

What do you envy?

Is it someone else's looks? Possessions? Family? Future? Spouse? Boyfriend or girlfriend? What specifically do you wish you had? Is there some way you could have any part of what you envy? If you could make a change that would allow you to have whatever it is you envy, would you actually make that change if you could? Why or why not?

293. Imagine that your family is going to be featured on a new reality show. How do you think the network should advertise the show? What should they say about your family? Write the press release describing the show.

294. What is one of the bravest things you have ever done? It just needs to be brave, for you. What takes great courage for one person may be quite easy for another.

295. Write a love letter to something that is not a human. Is it an animal? An item of clothing? An heirloom piece of furniture? Or...?

296.

Think of a character you know well, from a book, a television show, or a movie. Imagine that this character knows you and is mad at you. Why is he or she mad? What did you do? (Or what does he or she *think* you did?)

The character is letting you have it, telling you exactly how he or she feels. What does this character say?

Make the situation and the character's words as realistic as possible, based on what you know about the character. For example, Raymond on the old *Everybody Loves Raymond* show might be mad at you for telling his wife that he was playing golf instead of looking for a birthday present for the twins, as he had promised. Nemo, from the movie *Finding Nemo*, might be mad at you for telling his father he is right to be so overprotective. Scout, from the book *To Kill a Mockingbird*, might be mad at you for telling others about her special hiding place.

297. Write a confession. Who is making the confession? (It shouldn't be you.) Is it going to be a confession about something serious, something silly, something inconsequential, something that may have mattered more to the guilty party than to the party that was wronged? Or?

Why is the character going to confess? Is it a guilty conscience? Part of a plea bargain? A way to get some kind of revenge? Is the character going to mean what he or she says?

Write the confession in first person, as if you are the character confessing.

298. A Dr. Seuss character says, "I do not like green eggs and ham!" He doesn't like them anywhere, in any way, with anything. What do you not like anywhere, in any way, with anything? Explain.

299. Here's your title: *No One Cares.* Write a poem, a paragraph, or an essay that fits that title.

300.
Describe your first job. How old were you? What did you do? How were you hired? Were you successful? Explain. (If you haven't been hired for a job yet, think again. Are you sure? Have you ever been paid to do *anything*? If so, that was a job.)

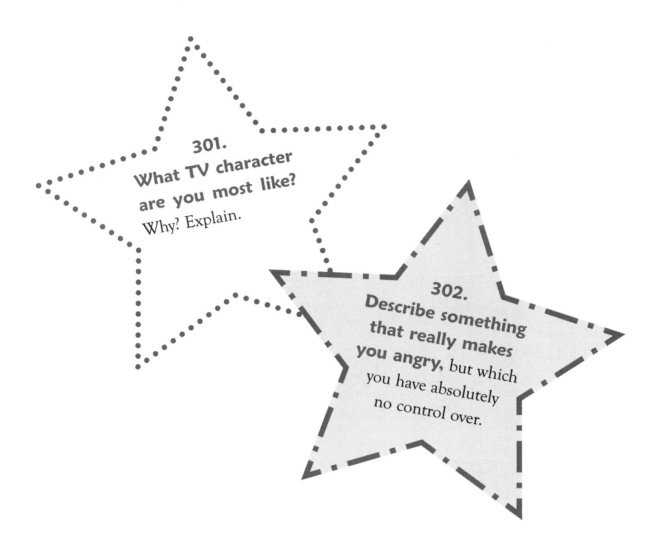

301.
What TV character are you most like? Why? Explain.

302.
Describe something that really makes you angry, but which you have absolutely no control over.

303. What do (or did) your parents just never understand about you? Explain.

304. What do (or did) you not understand about your parents? Explain.

305. Create a setting for a short story or a novel. Make the setting in another place and time. Where will it be? On another continent? On another planet? Another galaxy? Will it be set in the past or the future? Write one paragraph of the story or novel, making it clear in that paragraph when and where the story is taking place.

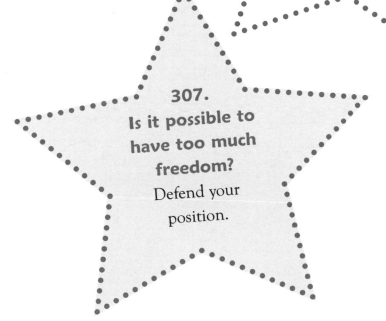

306.
What does freedom mean to you?

307.
Is it possible to have too much freedom?
Defend your position.

308.

How do you feel about compliments? Can you accept them easily, or do they embarrass you? Have you ever received a compliment that was not intended as a compliment but still made you feel great? Have you ever received a compliment you felt was insincere? Have you ever received a compliment that, for some reason, made you feel terrible? Do you compliment others easily? Do others in your life compliment you easily? Discuss.

309. **Do people today understand sacrifice?** What does *sacrifice* mean to you? Is it important? Is it relevant to your life? Has there ever been a time when you made a true sacrifice? Explain.

310. **Choose a character you know well,** from a book, a television show, or a movie. Write a diary entry for that character, for a holiday or special occasion. For example, you might write a diary entry for Harry Potter for Christmas Day, or the television character Raven for her birthday, or Romeo for Valentine's Day.

Write in first person, as if you *are* that character.

311. **Imagine a person who is trying hard not to fall asleep.** Where is the person? What is happening? Is the person sleepy because of what is happening, or for another reason?

In one paragraph, describe the person.

312. Ear worms are those little snatches of song that get stuck in your brain and drive you crazy. Have you ever paid attention to your ear worms? Do the same songs get stuck, time after time, or do different ones plop into your brain? Do they show up because you have heard them playing somewhere, perhaps as background music in a store? Have you ever had an ear worm triggered by something someone said? (For example, you heard a customer at a store say, "I need to see a manager. I'm just not getting satisfaction here!" Later you found yourself humming the chorus from the Rolling Stones song, "I can't get no satisfaction.")

Discuss your experience with ear worms.

313.

In the book *The Hitchhiker's Guide to the Galaxy*, characters are punished by having to listen to bad poetry. In a similar spirit, some coffee shops around the country are hosting a weekly Bad Poetry Night.

Try your hand at creating some bad poetry. Write the worst poem you can imagine.

You might choose an incredibly boring subject. You might carry on and on about something so personal that no one else could possibly be interested. You might write a rhyming poem with lines clearly chosen only because they fit the rhyme scheme, not the subject of the poem. You might be overly emotional, or choose old-fashioned, unnatural-sounding language.

Let your imagination run wild.

314.

All of us grow up hearing certain phrases or sayings repeated frequently by our parents, grandparents, or others close to us. For example, we might hear, "A penny saved is a penny earned," or "Hard work never hurt anybody," or "Don't be such a baby!" What sayings or phrases have you heard? Which ones have had the biggest impact on you? Have they molded your life in any way?

315. **One treatment for depression** involves having people give themselves credit, both verbally and in writing, for even the smallest accomplishments all day long. Many have said that the technique helps, even if they feel silly about it. They find it starts to change their thinking.

Think of your own day, yesterday. Imagine that you are complimenting yourself for every tiny hurdle you cleared all day long.

If you find it hard to get up in the morning, pat yourself on the back for getting up. If that's not hard for you, you might want to pat yourself on the back for choosing a healthy breakfast instead of the cookie and Coke you really wanted. You didn't want to shower, but you did anyway? Tell yourself, "Good job." Continue through the day, writing out at least 10 congratulatory notes to yourself.

316. **Pump up your list from #315 with the most interesting, descriptive details** you can think of. Instead of, "Good for me; I got out of bed," you might write, "Good for me. I pulled myself from under the cozy warmth of my comforter and rolled out into the harsh coldness of my underheated bedroom."

317. Paris Hilton is probably partly responsible for the popularity of "That's hot" as a favorable description of something. At the same time, "That's cool" is still a positive remark. Is "That's warm" next?

What if you could be the one to invent a slang phrase that caught on? Think of three words or phrases that you think would be appropriate. You might actually invent a new word, or you might use an existing word or phrase so that it has new meaning. Define your slang, and then use all three words or phrases in a paragraph that illustrates their meaning.

**318.
Write a lively description of something bland.**
(Ideas: rice cereal with milk, mashed potatoes, old reruns of "Lassie," a beige room, elevator music.) Though your subject is bland, make the description as interesting as possible by choosing your words carefully.

**319.
You've got a job writing Valentine cards.**
You've written hundreds of "Roses are red, violets are blue" poems. Now your boss wants you to do poems that involve other colors and plants, perhaps starting with "Daisies are yellow," or "Weeds are green." Write three more poems.

320. **Have you ever set a goal and reached it?** If so, what was it? Was it a seemingly small goal? An especially difficult goal? A financially rewarding goal? Or...? Describe what happened and how you felt.

If you have never set a goal and reached it, why do you think that is true? Explain.

321. **Many believe that "imagining" is the first step** in succeeding at something. If you can't imagine yourself doing something, so the philosophy goes, you can't possibly succeed at it.

For example, if a person wants to lose weight, he should first imagine himself as a thinner person. He should let the image of a thinner self knock about in his brain for a while, perhaps even before he starts to diet.

What do you think? Is imagining important? Why or why not? Has it ever succeeded for you?

322.
Some people go crazy when their clothes and hair are full of static. Some find that their skin crawls at the touch of a cotton ball. Some feel they will lose their mind when the wind blows their hair into their face or when someone scratches a fingernail against a blackboard.

How are you sensitive? What ordinary sensations make *you* crazy?

323.
Complete this sentence ten different ways:

Hope is...

324. Think of a political or social issue that interested you when you were younger. Were you worried about the homeless people you saw in the streets? Did you want to help starving children in Africa? Did you want to fight pollution? Run for president? Save an endangered species?

Think of a political or social issue that interests you today. Is it the same issue? If so, is your passion level the same as it used to be?

Is it a different issue? If so, do you still care about the first one? What does your change in interests have to say about how you have changed over the years? Explain.

**325.
Here is a basic, basic sentence:**

She expressed amusement.

Keeping the same meaning, rewrite the sentence so that it is *much* more interesting. Do not use the words *she, expressed* or *amusement*.

Who is *she?* Is she a mom, a model, a sky diver, the mayor, a teacher, a grandmother, or...? Does she *giggle, guffaw, smile,* or...? Why is she expressing amusement?

**326.
Write a conversation that involves a misunderstanding** of some kind. Don't introduce the characters. Just start the conversation, making it clear from the conversation what the misunderstanding is about. Try to make the characters speak as real people would speak.

327.

Choose a paragraph you have written—perhaps something you have written for one of the *Yoga for the Brain* exercises. Go through the paragraph and circle all the verbs. (Just to refresh your memory, verbs are words that express action. They also include "being" or "helping" verbs, such as *is, be, am, are, was, were, been, has, have, had, do, does, did, can, could, shall, should, will, would, may, might, must.*)

Now go back and replace all the verbs you circled with different ones. Try to find more expressive, interesting verbs than you used in your original. Or, for a different approach, choose verbs that change the tone or impression of your original paragraph. For example, if you wrote that someone *exploded* with laughter, you might change the impression by saying that person *leaked* a giggle. Experiment!

328. He's not bald. He's follicly deprived. She's not short. She is vertically challenged. The puppy didn't die. It joined its mommy and daddy in that steak-filled doggie run in the sky.

Write a paragraph full of euphemisms that go to ridiculous lengths not to offend.

329. Do you have a superstition or unusual belief? For example, one musician believes that she won't play well unless she drinks a root beer before a performance. A man secretly believes that the devil records all of the things you say that you hate during your lifetime, so that he can create a personalized version of hell for you after you die. A small business owner believes that if she makes her bed and closes all the closet doors before she goes to work, the mailman will deliver envelopes full of customer payments.

> **330.**
> Complete this sentence ten different ways:
>
> **Disappointment is...**

Describe unusual beliefs or superstitions you have or have heard about. Why do you think people develop superstitions?

331. You are pitching your idea for a new television series to a network executive. The network has given you 100 words or less to describe the show. Which network is it? What is the show? Make your pitch.

332. **Write three different sentences, each using the word** *crushed.* Create an entirely different image with each sentence.

333. **It's the final moments of a beauty pageant.** The judges ask Veronica Gazelle what she hopes to accomplish with her life. She replies, "I want to promote world peace."

The judges ask contestant Emily Lithe the same question. She answers, "I want to help make sure all the little children in the universe have enough to eat every night before their little heads hit their pillows—and I want to make sure they have pillows, too."

Finally, the judges ask Cecilia Straightshooter the same question. Cecilia, however, tells the absolute truth, and at length. What does she say?

334.
What do you wish you knew a whole lot more about?
Why? Explain.

335.

Harriet has a little problem with assertiveness. She is not able to say what she means with much emphasis or clarity. For example, here's what she told her neighbor:

Leonard, I know that you really, really loved your Doberman pinscher, and I don't mind the 20-foot statue you had made of Fluffy for your backyard, even though it pretty much cuts off my view of the mountains, unless I stand on my patio and climb up on the grill and lean way to the east. I don't even mind the lights you attached last week all that much, as long as I close all my drapes. And I know it would probably help, too, if I got some room-darkening shades.

I don't even mind the "Doggie Woggie" hip-hop song you wrote and recorded with that group from downtown, at least not all that much, except maybe at 3:00 a.m. after about the 515th time I've heard it coming out of your memorial loud speaker.

However, I'd kind of appreciate it if you would do some adjusting with the memorial recording of Fluffy's bark, which I know was very precious to you, but which is not quite so precious to others. The bark recording is on automatic sensors, so that the movement of a squirrel sets it off, but, you know, you've got a lot of squirrels out there, so poor departed Fluffy is pretty much barking all of the time. I'm wondering if I could trouble you to maybe set the Fluffy sensor back a little, so that Fluffy barks after every 50th squirrel goes by? I hate to be a bother, but I hope I can trouble you to make some changes. Please?

Rewrite Harriet's speech to her neighbor, so that she is much more clear and assertive about what she wants, without being rude.

336. You're running for president of the United States. You and your advisors have decided that the American public can focus on only one issue at a time. You have one sentence to communicate something really important about what you believe, or how you are going to run the country, or how you are going to make things better. What is your sentence going to be? Craft it carefully.

337. Which would you rather watch—a NASCAR race, a 20-yard dash, a marathon, a horse race, a dog race, or a three-legged race? Why? Explain.

338. Tell someone off. Don't say who. Just give them a piece of your mind, in writing, in a letter you will never send. Express yourself with strong, but not foul, language. Vent, vent, vent!

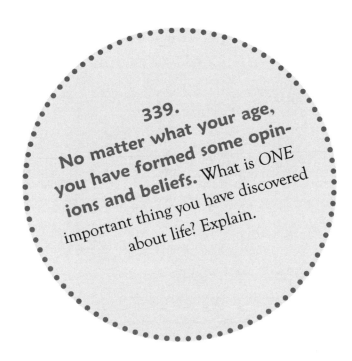

339. No matter what your age, you have formed some opinions and beliefs. What is ONE important thing you have discovered about life? Explain.

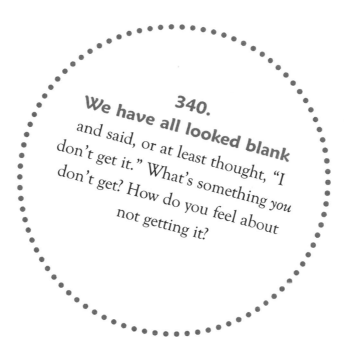

340.
We have all looked blank and said, or at least thought, "I don't get it." What's something you don't get? How do you feel about not getting it?

341. **Give at least three reasons of support for something utterly ridiculous**—the more ridiculous, the better. (Examples: Give three reasons why stores should charge customers to enter. Give three reasons why children should not be allowed, ever, to ride bicycles. Give three reasons why every homeowner should be required to keep a fish.)

342. **Make a list of things that have wheels**—skateboards, strollers, Humvees, vacuum cleaners, lawn mowers, etc. Then write a poem called "Wheels."

Your poem can rhyme, or not. It must include at least one simile. (A simile is a comparison that creates an image or picture and uses the words *like* or *as*. Example: *His feet in their new running shoes looked like Volkswagen bugs parked at the end of his legs.*)

343. Write a paragraph describing a modern-day Scrooge in action. Does this Scrooge have employees? If so, what kind of business is it? What does he do to upset his employees?

In one paragraph, help us see what Scrooge is like, without *telling* us what he is like. For example, instead of saying, "Scrooge is cheap," let readers draw that conclusion for themselves by saying, "Scrooge checked desk drawers every night, to be sure no one had taken a box of paper clips out of the storage cabinet before he absolutely needed it."

344. What "Chris" do you most resemble—Christopher Columbus, Kris Kringle, KRISpy Kreme doughnuts, Kris Kristofferson, CHRIStie Brinkley, CHRIStopher Walken, CHRIStina Aguilera? (You may have to do some research if you don't recognize some of these names.) Explain.

345. Write about a secret. Is there a secret that had a big effect on you when you discovered it? Has someone ever broken a promise not to tell one of your secrets? Have you ever kept a secret you shouldn't have kept? Are secrets ever a good thing? Why or why not?

346.

What do you have doubts about? Is it about a decision you have made? Is it about something you have always believed, or think you should believe? Is it about whether or not to trust someone? Or...?

---

347. **No one can know everything.** Still, most of us are embarrassed when we find we don't know something others know. One woman was shocked to discover the word *chic* is not pronounced "chick." (Unfortunately, she discovered her error by saying the word incorrectly in front of her older brother, who did not exactly react with sensitivity.) A man found out, the hard way, that you shouldn't use nylon cord to truss the Thanksgiving turkey. (It melted over the bird.) When planning to see his six-week-old twin nephews for the first time, a teenage boy remarked that, "They should have their eyes open by then." (His father dissolved in laughter. "They're not puppies!" he laughed.)

When have you been embarrassed to find that you didn't know something? What happened?

348. **How many "ink" words can you use in one paragraph?** Use *pink, wink, brink, sink, wrinkle,* and as many other words as possible that have "ink" in them.

349.
Write a letter to the manufacturer, explaining why you are returning the *klorpindoodle* you ordered. If you like, you can throw in a complaint about what is wrong with the *snorfishelbopper* you ordered at the same time. (You ordered these items, so of course you know what they are and why you wanted them!)

350.

Mark Twain wrote, "The difference between the right word and nearly the right word is the same as that between lightning and lightning bug."

What are the right words for telling your friend that you think the outfit she bought is the ugliest, most unflattering outfit you have ever seen anyone wear, anywhere, at any time? She's asking what you think.

Are you tempted to lie? She needs this outfit for a very special occasion. Do you really want to send her out in the world looking terrible? What words can you use to tell her the truth, but kindly?

Or do you believe that the "right" words, in this case, would be untrue words? Are her feelings more important than the truth?

351. **You have been given the opportunity of a lifetime.** You have been asked to write the movie sequel to *King Kong*. All you have been told is that the movie will be called *Queen Quang*. You get to decide everything else.

The first thing the studio wants is a description of the character Queen Quang, so they can start designing it/him/her. Write your description.

352.
When people describe Cecilia, they always say, "She's such a character." Who have you known who is a character? Describe him or her.

353. **Write a paragraph** made up entirely of three-syllable words. How long can you make it?

354. **Finish this sentence three different ways,** creating a different feeling with each sentence:

Nigel couldn't believe his eyes when...

355.

Drew's teachers keep nagging him about sentence fragments. He always seems to leave out something, and his work seems to sputter along in short, incomplete bursts.

Here are some of his recent sentence fragments. Turn them into complete sentences. (Yes, you could complete some of them by adding only a word or two, but go beyond that. Really flesh out the sentences and make them *interesting.*)

* when Lulu's elastic broke
* ignoring the warning sign
* by the time the Civil War reenactment group showed up
* after the explosive sound from the kitchen
* because of his hypochondria
* tackling the quarterback
* over the river and through the woods to Grandmother's house at the end of the cul-de-sac
* the sticky peppermint that was stuck to the back of the suede leather jacket
* next to the girl who was next to the girl he really wanted to be next to
* around the time of the extinction of the dodo bird

356.

Limericks can be funny, off-color, or even downright dirty. Try your hand at writing a G-rated, squeaky clean limerick.

Here's an example:

There once was a hippo named Pam.
Who sat eating lunch on the dam.
    When she finished her cake,
    She heard the dam break,
and said, "Why'd I eat the whole ham?"

Here are a few guidelines for writing limericks:

• They generally follow a meter (or rhythm) something like this:

da DUM da da DUM da da DUM
da DUM da da DUM da da DUM
    da DUM da da DUM
    da DUM da da DUM
da DUM da da DUM da da DUM

• They often begin by telling a character's name or where the character is from (as in "There was a young soldier named Lee," or "There once was a woman from France").
• They often involve a joke of some kind.
• The first, second, and fifth lines rhyme with each other.
  The third and fourth lines rhyme with each other.

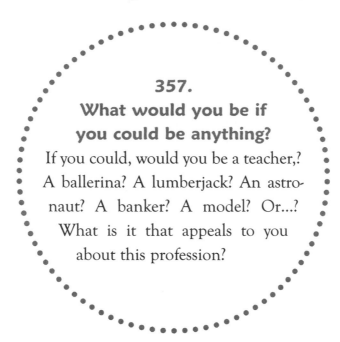

357.

What would you be if you could be anything?

If you could, would you be a teacher,? A ballerina? A lumberjack? An astronaut? A banker? A model? Or...? What is it that appeals to you about this profession?

358. Five individuals are each preparing a snack. The five are:

- a college student in the dorm
- a stay-at-home mom or dad
- a chef
- a child
- a backpacker in the woods

Create a vivid picture of what each individual is doing, using one sentence for each.

359. Your family has offered to spoil you. They aren't going to buy you expensive gifts. What are they going to do? Describe how you will be spoiled.

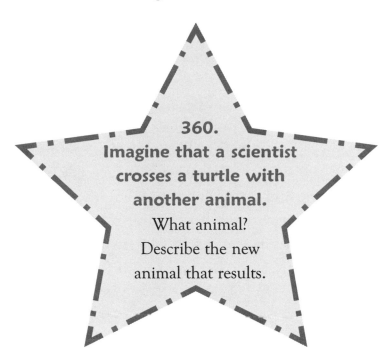

360.
Imagine that a scientist crosses a turtle with another animal.
What animal?
Describe the new animal that results.

361. **We have all seen commercials that tug at our hearts,** perhaps even bringing a tear to our eyes, even though they are for something unsentimental like phone service or credit cards. Write a tear-jerking commercial for one of the following:

- an antacid
- a vacuum cleaner
- an umbrella.

362. **You are on a road trip in a Winnebago** with family members. Someone has invited a friend along. In your opinion, that is turning out to be the mistake of the century. This person, in your opinion, is the most annoying person in the universe.

Who is this person? What, precisely, is he or she doing that drives you nuts? Explain, so that *anyone* will sympathize with you.

363.

In an old Calvin and Hobbes comic strip, Calvin announces, "I like to verb words." "Verbing" words is, in fact, quite common in our language. People take perfectly good adjectives and nouns and turn them into verbs, as in "She's going to *office* out of her home."

Or, suppose someone said, "Clyde *flamingoed* his lawn." A perfectly good noun, flamingo, is turned into a verb. Though "flamingoed" may never have been used as a verb before, anywhere, you probably have a pretty good idea of what Clyde did. (Just picture those pink plastic flamingoes stuck in the front of the flower bed.)

Try some verbing of your own. Write sentences that use each of these nouns in a new way, as verbs:

- giraffe
- nature
- saxophone
- tooth
- basketball

Then choose another noun and write a sentence using it, in a new way, as a verb.

364.

Paula told her mother why she came home from her friend's house without any shoes. "Mrs. Angelo's cat fell in the hot tub," she explained.

Clearly, Paula was leaving out a few things. When her mother called Mrs. Angelo, she got the whole story: The cat fell in the hot tub. It was terrified and scrambled to get out, but couldn't. When Mrs. Angelo grabbed him, the cat scratched her so deeply on the arm that she saw she needed to go to the emergency room for stitches. Because she couldn't leave the children alone, she put them in the car wearing only their bathing suits and headed for the hospital.

When they returned from the hospital, Paula's shoes had been eaten by Mrs. Angelo's new puppy, who had become so agitated hearing the cat yowl and Mrs. Angelo scream that she had grabbed the first thing she could find to chew on—Paula's shoes.

And that's why Paula had no shoes on when she came home.

Below are three questions, each followed by an answer that clearly leaves out some important details. Fill in those details.

- Why did her son fail algebra? It's because her lipstick melted in its case.
- Why did the garbage disposal malfunction? It's because Nick broke his leg skiing.
- Why did the car overheat? It's because Audrey left her Barbie doll outside overnight.

365. **Here are some famous first lines from novels:**

- "As Gregor Samsa awoke that morning from uneasy dreams he found himself transformed in his bed into a gigantic insect. (*The Metamorphosis,* by Franz Kafka)

- "It was the best of times, it was the worst of times..." (A *Tale of Two Cities,* by Charles Dickens)

- "Happy families are all alike; every unhappy family is unhappy in its own way." (*Anna Karenina,* by Leo Tolstoy)

- "Call me Ishmael." (*Moby Dick,* by Herman Melville)

- "It was a bright cold day in April, and the clocks were striking thirteen." (*1984,* by George Orwell)

- "When he was nearly thirteen, my brother Jem got his arm badly broken at the elbow." (*To Kill a Mockingbird,* by Harper Lee)

- In my younger and more vulnerable years my father gave me some advice that I've been turning over in my mind ever since." (*The Great Gatsby,* by F. Scott Fitzgerald)

Choose *three* of the lines and incorporate them into a paragraph that might begin a new novel.

And finally...a bonus question, for leap year:

366.
What does the world
need more of, besides,
"love, sweet love"?

Real-World Writing Projects

Real-World Writing Projects

Real-World Writing Projects can vary tremendously. The only requirements are these:

- that the results be shared with others. (If you are doing a project as part of a class, your teacher doesn't count as "others.")
- that they have some real use in your life.
- that they involve writing in some way.

The ideas that follow are in no way meant to be definitive. Feel free to use any of these ideas, or to adapt them to your own needs, but also feel free to create your own project idea. Choose something that you will enjoy doing, or that you can imagine someone else enjoying when they read it.

1.   **Create a sports video, with narration.** Videotape a friend or relative's sports events for a season and create an edited videotape of highlights. Then write a voice-over for the tape. You might want to write it as a sports announcer calling all the plays, or you might want to do something quite original.

For example, you could write narration in the form of a fairy tale: *Once upon a time there was a volleyball player who decided to battle the big, bad Wolverines...*

Or you could write it as a lighthearted commercial, "selling" someone as a potential recruit. *(For a quarterback who will lead your team to victory, look no further than Emory Feldspar.)*

Or you could write it as a mystery: *The private detective knew he had a big job ahead of him. How did the Seneca Stallions manage to beat the Airedale Avengers for the third year in a row, despite the fact that all the starters had graduated the year before? He pulled out footage of the games...*

Whatever format you decide on, show the video at the end of the season, and give it as a gift to the featured player (or players).

2.   **Write a thank-you letter to someone who will be very surprised to receive it**. Thank someone for something she did, whether she knew it or not, that really affected you in a positive way—even if it didn't seem so positive at the time. The thank-you does not have to be for a huge, life-changing action. It might be for only a simple kindness that you appreciated more than you ever let on.

Just a few ideas: You might thank a teacher who didn't give up on you, an employer who gave you your first chance at a job, a neighbor who listened to you when you needed help, a relative who always had time for you.

Another idea is to thank someone for what he is doing right now. For example, you might write a thank-you letter to a friend who always tells you the truth, even when you don't want to hear it, or to a relative who always sees when you need a little bit of a push or a helping hand, and then gives you that push or that helping hand. You might thank a spouse for sticking with you through a tough time, or a child for facing a difficulty with courage. You might even surprise a brother or sister with a thank-you for lending you a favorite item of clothing, or for not telling on you when it would have been tempting to do so.

3. **Write a letter to the editor of a newspaper on a subject you find important.** The letters to the editor section is one of the most popular and most widely read pages of most newspapers. Take advantage of its popularity. Do you want others to support a certain political candidate? Do you want to change something about a local school? Do you want others to support a worthy cause? With a well-reasoned letter to the editor, make a point that might actually swing others to your point of view.

4. **Make an "All about _____" newsletter for babysitters.** Create a newspaper about your child, grandchild, or little brother or sister. Be sure to include all kinds of helpful information—emergency numbers, of course, but don't stop there. Has the child recently learned to open drawers or communicate something in sign language? Does he or she have allergies? What foods does he or she particularly love? Do you have any hints for getting the child to go to sleep? Is there anything you should caution the babysitter about?

    Store the newsletter on your computer so that you can change it frequently as the child grows or details change. Then you can print out an up-to-the-minute copy whenever you expect a babysitter.

    On page 121 are the first three pages of a four-page newsletter Heather Stenner of Fort Collins, Colorado, uses for her daughter Emma.

THE EMMA HERALD

November 13–14, 2004

The night her parents left her for the very first time

Emma Charlene Stenner
Birthdate: June 8, 2003
Eyes: Green/Brown
Height: 29.5 inches
Weight: 17.5 lbs
Shoe Size: 3
Smile: Terrific!

Inside this issue:

Her Medical Info   2

What's there to eat?   2

Emma Favorites!   2

An ordinary day   3

Another kind of day   3

Sleep Patterns   3

Emma Dos/Don'ts   4

Diaper Duty

That girl can climb!

Well, mom and dad have hit the road and Aunt Sandy and Grandma are taking care of that crazy red-head!

We're all wondering what new trick she'll master this weekend. The learning curve is big but she always seems to face it head on.

The biggest news is that Emma is climbing! Not just climbing up a few pillows, but into her high-chair all by herself as well as any other chair that might be available.

In the bathroom, she has learned how to move the brown stool to the sink and climb onto that to get whatever she needs. She learned this when mom wanted her to brush her teeth. You don't want to leave anything on the sink that would not be for little girls hands!

She's also climbing onto the chairs by the kitchen table. This makes for very interesting times when art projects are being worked on my mom.

Now, if there is any outdoor time at the park, this girl flies. No lifting needed. Emma likes to do it all herself. She's been known to push her mom's hand away when she was trying to spot her up a big climb. She does seem to have a kind of natural way of knowing that something's just too hard for her. She'll usually just come back down and try something else that's more her style.

Keep your eye on her. She's FAST!!!!

"I think I'll climb Mt. Everest in my free time next year! –Emma

Emergency Contact Numbers

- Call 911 if anything major happens!
- Call 204 –0300 to contact someone at Associates in

Show me that sign!

The ability to communicate is so powerful and that's why it's so nice to do something new, you can count on Emma for using all the signs she's

These are a few of the most commonly used signs by Emma

The Emma Herald

Her Medical Information

Doctor: Dr. Colleen McCreery
Associates in Family Medicine
3519 Richmond Drive
Phone: 970-204-0300
HOURS: 8 a.m -9 p.m. Everyday
Insurance is through Pacificare
They have her insurance card on file.

Allergies: Penicillin
No food allergies yet.

Directions to the AFM Doctor's office:

Get on Taft and go South.

Turn left and go East on Horsetooth.

Turn left before the Conoco station at Shields and Horsetooth. It's on your left. Associates in Family Medicine.

See Doc!
I'm getting lots of new teeth!

Sandy Brooks has my written permission to act as guardian for Emma Stenner in case of an emergency.

11-12-04 Heather Stenner

What's there to eat?

While you're here, please make yourself at home. Whatever's in the fridge is fair game. There's also a pantry above the washing machine. Lots of snacks in there too.

Emma's been doing a great job of eating lately. She likes vegetables and cheese a lot. She's drinking milk and for snack it's ok to mix one of her red juice cans with some milk in her sippy cup.

We're also really trying to get her to eat good helpings of meat.

Cottage Cheese is always a fav! She drinks OJ for breakfast only. And

milk is the only thing she gets to drink with meals. The doctor doesn't really want us to offer her water in large amounts.

She's also getting to be big enough that she doesn't need the little spill guard in the lid when she is in her highchair. She seems to get more down easier when it's not it. She'll love it if you can have while she's eating. Just make sure she keeps eating!

Sometimes when she's done she'll start pushing food off her high-chair. Just ignore that and ask her

to show you a sign for what she wants. Hopefully she'll sign all done. You could ask her if she wants some ice cream for dessert. Usually that gets a big Uh huh!

To get her to finish something on her plate or get her started eating again, you can ask her if you can have some. Either she'll offer to share it with you or she'll play a little game where she pretends to give it to you and then snatches it up for herself!

Emma's Favorite Things   (at least for today!)

A Pencil and Paper (You can substitute a pen or crayon)
The right-handed one-year old has made her mark! Emma has been known to write essays on the effects of pomegranates on babies. Just last week she was penning over a tablet given to her by the local Longs Drugstore.

We're not sure if she knows what she's doing but she sure seems to enjoy the details. If you get right down on the floor and draw with her, you might end up there for hours!

Dancing While on the Telephone Holding her Bear
For some reason, she has fallen in love with Bears! She's loved the telephone since she was a few months old. Bottom line: She loves to dance to music. Put them all together and there you go! 1 happy girl!

Her Sign Language Video
She has always loved to watch her sign language video. Sit with her if you like. Watch her watch it. Simply observing how much she can do on her own is awesome!

An Ordinary Day in the life of Emma (2 naps)

6:30 to 7:00 a.m. She wakes up with a soakin' wet diaper. Sometimes poopy.

7:00 a.m. BREAKFAST

7:20 –10 or 10:30 PLAYTIME GALORE!

10:30 to 12:30 or longer! NAPTIME

12:30 or 1:00—LUNCH

1:00 PLAYTIME!

4 or 4:30 Another chance to NAP

5:30 or 6 Up for SUPPER

6:30 to 7:45 PLAYTIME

7:45 to 8:15 BATHTIME

8:00 to 8:30 BOOKS AND BEDTIME.
We read in the spare bedroom or on the couch in the living room.

The other Ordinary Day in the life of Emma (1 nap)

6:30 to 7:00 a.m. She wakes up with a soakin' wet diaper. Sometimes poopy.

7:00 a.m. BREAKFAST

7:20 PLAYTIME GALORE/Get ready to go leave

9 or 10 She'll have a class or a friend over to play

11:30 or 12:00 noon —LUNCH

12:30 p.m. NAPTIME

2 or 3 p.m. PLAYTIME!

5:30 or 6 Up for SUPPER

6:30 to 7:45 PLAYTIME

7:45 to 8:15 BATHTIME

8:00 to 8:30 BOOKS AND BEDTIME.
We read in the spare bedroom or on the couch in the living room.

Sleep Patterns

Whether you are putting Emma down to rest for a nap or for the night, she usually has no problem. She knows the sign for sleep and sometimes will even ask to lay down in her crib.

*Have the humidifier filled up BEFORE you lay her down.
*Close the curtains in her room.
*Of course, it's good to check that diaper 1st (At nighttime make sure to use a night diaper) and then just tell her it's time to rest for a while.

*Try not to make a big deal about going to sleep. It's just something we do right? So I lay her in the crib with her pacifier and blanket and after kisses and I love yous, I turn out the light, (there is a night light in there) and close the door. AT NIGHTTIME: Whenever you go to bed, you will want to go in and cover her up and leave the door open so it stays a little warmer in there over night.

*Usually she will go right to sleep. HOWEVER....

There are a few times when:
She will throw her pacifier and/or blanket over the edge. If she is not quieting down in 10 minutes I go in and without much talking I hand her the pacifier and blanket give her a hug in the crib and tell her she needs to get some rest. Then I leave her again.

OR... Sometimes at naptime, she will poop after you put her in her crib. Maybe 5 or 10 minutes after you put her in there she will be talking and/or whining. Just go in and with a minimum amount of talking, to try and keep her quieted down, I change her diaper (BE PREPARED... they are pretty bad these days!!!) and then I just lay her back down to sleep.

She will also wake up during the night and make sounds, usually we just have to go in and cover her up and that's all it takes. If she actually wakes up, we usually change her diaper and then rock her back to sleep in the rocking chair.

---

5. **Create a whole line of original greeting cards**. Make cards for every occasion you can imagine, designing the covers and writing original greetings for the inside of each.

    Do you want to write your greetings as poems? As simple statements that reflect sentiments? Do you want a theme for the whole line? Maybe you want a "cat" theme, a "truck" theme, or a "sports heroes," theme, for example.

    Give a box of the cards as a gift, or save the cards to use yourself.

6. **Submit an article or a short story for publication.** Before you send your piece off to an editor, do your homework. Check the reference book *Writer's Market* for details about where to send your submission. It lists hundreds of publications, their editors, and details about the kinds of things they publish.

    Another idea is to go to a publisher's web site. You can usually find writers' guidelines, if the company does accept unsolicited submissions. (Some do not. Others accept submissions only from agents.)

    It is a good idea to submit only to publications you have actually read. If you have read a publication, you have a better idea of the kind of material it is looking for.

    If you are a young person, you may want to limit yourself to publications (both print and online) that look for material by children or teens. A few such publications are *Stone Soup Magazine, Teen Voices, Teen Ink, Skipping Stones* and the web site www.kidpub.com.

7. **Create an "According to Our Family" keepsake.** Come up with a question you think is interesting and which you could ask relatives of all ages. A few examples:

- What do you remember about your first day of school?
- What were your favorite games or toys when you were little?
- What is one of the best gifts you ever received?
- Who was your very first friend? Tell about him or her.
- What is your very first memory? Describe it.

Ask your question to all your relatives. You might mail or e-mail the question and ask for a written response. You might ask relatives in person, recording their answers to transcribe later. You might phone them and take notes as they answer. (Be sure to explain that you are collecting responses from the whole family for a booklet.)

Collect all the responses and then compile them, along with your own response, into a booklet. Add an introduction, telling about the project. (Perhaps you can include humorous anecdotes about collecting the information, or make some observations about the responses.) Be sure to list all contributors, their whole names, and the years of their birth. (Your book could well become a family keepsake, and people years from now may not have any idea who "Molly" is, unless you identify her with more than just a first name.) Another nice idea is to add childhood photos of each person.

Make copies of the booklet for all participants, as a gift for Christmas or some other special occasion. If the project is successful, you may want to follow up in future years with other booklets, using different questions.

8. **Write a prayer or affirmation.** If it fits with your religion or spiritual beliefs, write a prayer or affirmation that fits your own daily personal needs. Make it succinct, yet sincere. Keep a copy next to your bed, in your desk, or in your purse or backpack. If you find it comforting or helpful in any way, take the further step of sharing it with someone else.

Even better, create a booklet of prayers or affirmations for someone you know would appreciate it.

9. **Write a hip-hop number to perform at a special event**, as a gift or part of the entertainment. If you like hip-hop music, you will enjoy giving it a try yourself. If you hate it, don't worry. You may be shocked at how much fun you will have.

For example, Judy Reid of Breckenridge, Colorado, had a ball writing a hip-hop number for a friend's birthday party last year. Both Reid and her friend raise guide dog puppies, so she decided to write "Puppy Raiser Rap." She even performed the piece herself, along with some friends, and they were the hit of the party. Here are excerpts from the number she wrote:

Puppy Raiser Rap

Hey, now, we have this little rap we'd like to do for you.
We really haven't a clue, so please don't boo.
In fact, we feel like dunces, so don't all clap at onces…

Well, let me tell you a story about this puppy raisin' thing.
It ain't no joke, and it ain't no fling.
It ain't ducky soupy.
In fact, it's rather poopy.

Some people say that puppy raisin's totally cool.
Yeah, cool, pickin' up stools.
Yeah, cool, wipin' up drool.
Yeah, cool, cryin' like a fool.

So you get this little pup at two months old.
She's yours to cuddle, nurture, and mold.
But just about the time you hopelessly bond,
Guess what! The puppy's gone.
Yeah, gone, totally gone...

The song goes on to tell about how hard it is to give their puppies up once their training period is complete, and how rewarding it is to know they have raised a fine pet who will help someone someday.

When you create a hip-hop song, you can use one of the rhythms on a synthesizer, if you have one, for your accompaniment. Another idea is to use a hip-hop rhythm track CD, without lyrics. (Cottonwood Press, Inc., for example, sells one called "Rap-Rap-Rapsody," with 26 tracks.) You could also create and record your own rhythm sounds with drums, trash cans, etc. Possibilities are endless.

So are subjects!

10. **Create a "What They Said" Gift.** At a special event, such as a graduation, a baby or wedding shower, a wedding, or a birthday party, write down things people say. (An easy way to do this is to videotape the event and then extract interesting things as you watch later.) Try to note who said what.

Then write an interesting summary of the event and print it, using an attractive font. Attach it at the top of a poster board or a large sheet of paper. (If you can, get paper or poster board from an art store in a standard size for easy framing.) Then print out interesting things people said at the event, perhaps using different fonts and different colors. Paste them all onto the paper in an interesting collage. You might also want to add photographs from the event.

Frame the collage as a special, one-of-a-kind gift. Or take your collage to a photocopy center and have a color copy made. (This way, once your creation is complete, you won't have to worry about pieces coming unglued or falling off.) Then frame the copy.

11. **Write a "This I Believe" submission for National Public Radio.** National Public Radio (NPR) has a feature called "This I Believe," which is based on a 1950s radio program by acclaimed journalist Edward R. Murrow. People from all walks of life submit essays about the core beliefs that guide their daily lives. Those chosen are then invited to read their essays on the air.

    NPR has guidelines at its web site (www.npr.org) for submitting an essay. Think about what *you* believe, and submit an essay for the program.

12. **Write a resume**. If you have never written a resume and are interested in finding a job, writing a resume is a perfect project. On one page of paper, you will need to reflect as much as possible about you, in a positive way.

    There are dozens of references and guides to creating a resume, and there is no one, perfect model. You can find many guides to formatting on the Internet, and Microsoft Word even includes some resume templates in its program.

    What is more important than the format is what you say in your resume. Tell what you can do for a company, not what the company can do for you. If you haven't had a job before, describe what you *have* done. Did you lead a school club? Volunteer for your church? Play the lead in the school play? See if you can show some skills you have, even if you have never been paid for using those skills.

13. **Create a book for a special child in your life.** You might write and illustrate an original story. You might create a modern twist to a classic tale. You might write a nonfiction book about the child himself. (You could gather photographs and add explanations to create an "All About Jeremy" book, or a book called "Jeremy's Adventures," for example.) Take advantage of digital photography, computer programs like PhotoShop, and photocopy centers to create a one-of-a-kind masterpiece.

14. **Write love letters.** For special gifts like graduations, birthdays, weddings, etc., write love letters to people who are important to you. Tell them at least five reasons why you love and/or appreciate them. Remember special times you have had together. Write what you hope the future holds. Write or type your letter on nice paper, roll it up, and tie a ribbon around it. It is sure to be a gift that will be remembered.

15. **Create David Letterman-style "Top Ten" lists as gifts.** Letterman's television show features a "top ten" list nearly every night, always starting with item #10 and moving up to #1. Copy that format for some interesting gifts. For example, you might create the "Top Ten Best Pieces of Advice for Newlyweds," or "Top Ten Tips for Loving a Newborn," or "Top Ten Best Ways to Survive Your First Semester at College," or "Top Ten Ways to Succeed in Middle School." The best gifts usually have a combination of gentle teasing, humor, sweetness, and practicality.

16. **Create a pet book.** Possibilities abound for a book about pets. You might collect family pet stories and combine them with pictures of pets your family has had through the years. You might create a whole book about a certain pet, perhaps an especially pampered pet, and relate anecdotes about the pet, or tell of adventures with the pet over the years.

17. **Keep a travel journal.** On your next vacation or family trip, bring along an empty notebook or journal. Every night, write about what you did that day, but do more than just write a summary of events. Write your thoughts and observations about that day as well. Try to capture the details that can easily be forgotten after you return home.

    When you return home, combine excerpts from your journal with photos from the trip, ticket stubs, subway maps, dinner menus, and other mementos to create an interesting scrapbook to share with others. Such a scrapbook can be much more interesting than an album full of photos or a slide show online. By adding comments and remarks about your travel, you can make the trip seem much more real to others.

18. **Write a holiday newspaper.** Instead of writing a letter, summarize your family's year newspaper style, complete with headlines and stories written in third-person. In other words, give information as if you are a reporter, as in "Samantha Fieldstone, youngest daughter of John and Lisa Fieldstone, played the role of a tree in McCauley Elementary School's production of *Our Wonderful Forest.*"

    Don't forget to include photos and captions. You may want to have a story about every member of your family, including the pets. You may want a sports page, a comic strip, a food section with a favorite family recipe, or even an editorial. Try to make the newspaper truly interesting, without being "braggy."

    On page 129 is the front page of one family newspaper, courtesy of Chris Markuson of Pueblo, Colorado.

HAPPY NEW YEAR!

THE Holiday Herald
DECEMBER 2003

Merry Christmas!

Sophia enjoys being girly

PUEBLO, COLO. — Unbeknownst to her tomboy mother and Aunt Lizzy and her adventure-seeking Aunt Natalie, Sophia entered the world as a "girly" girl.

Sophia loves pink and purple. She thinks she is a princess and loves to wear jewelry. She is often found taking off outfits that involve pants and T-shirts to sneak on a dress. (She also calls all of her dresses "wonderfuls.")

While her mother and aunts would rather die than play with Barbie, Sophia is a full-fledged fan of the disproportioned doll. In fact, Sophia only likes to play with dolls and puppies.

We do scratch our heads in puzzlement about where this dainty little girl came from, but we don't mind. We love our sassy little Queen Bee-in-training.

Max, in the front, contemplates victory.

Max plays football

PUEBLO, COLO. — At 36 pounds and 39-inches tall, Max stood tall on the Pee Wee football field this fall.

Unlike most of "big" boys who were 5-years-old and owned football pants and cleats, Max started the football season a pure football novice. As an example of his ignorance to football machismo, Max hugged and kissed one of his teammates at practice. He also stopped in the middle of a play to comment on the beautiful sunset to his dad.

Despite Max's lack of finesse and skill in the world of Pee Wee football, he loved it. In fact, Max, who often sees the world through melancholy glasses, attained 100% sheer bliss on the football field. Pure Nirvana! He also got to play quarterback for a whole quarter.

When you are in Pueblo, please drop in.
We would love to catch up with old friends.

Sophie is pretty in pink.

19. **Write a guest editorial for a newspaper.** Do you have strong opinions on a subject? Do you have more to say than you can say in a letter to the editor? A guest editorial may be the answer. Many local newspapers welcome guest editorials, especially if they are well-written and present a clear point of view.

   Newsweek magazine has a column called "My Turn," where readers can submit essays. (There is also a contest for high school students. Find details at www.newsweekeducation.com.) Large newspapers like the *New York Times* solicit opinion pieces for their editorial pages. Some newspapers, such as the *Denver Post*, even choose a panel of editorial writers each year, choosing people who represent a wide range of opinions.

   It is important to remember that your chance of being selected for publication is very small, given the number of submissions. However, you never know. Your piece may be just the original viewpoint a newspaper or magazine is looking for.

   If your editorial is not selected, don't give up. Try for smaller publications, such as a local organization's newsletter or a school or university publication.

20. **Write a letter to your senator or representative.** Writing your senators or representatives is an excellent writing opportunity, with the added benefit of having a chance to influence their opinion or actions. Legislators *do* listen to the people in their districts. No, they may not rush to do exactly what you suggest, but your opinion will be noted, and you will probably get an answer as well, either from an aid or from the actual senator or representative. Public opinion does influence legislators, and the only way for your opinion to be heard is to send it.

   Be sure your letter includes facts, not just emotional appeal. Verify that your "facts" are correct, too.

21. **Write an autobiography.** Writing an autobiography can be an extremely rewarding experience, whether you are 12 or 80. (If you're 12, it will probably be shorter!) It is generally easiest to write chronologically, from birth (or *before* your birth) until the present. Photos, with captions, make wonderful additions, as well as copies of report cards, ribbons, certificates, etc.

    There are many wonderful books on the market about writing autobiographies. They generally provide questions and writing prompts that will help you remember, as well as suggestions for how to put your book together. (Two possibilities are *Writing Your Life (for adults)* and *Writing Your Life (for young people)*, both by Mary Borg and published by Cottonwood Press, Inc.)

22. **Help someone else write an autobiography.** How much do you really know about the life of your mother, your father, your grandmother, or your grandfather? If information about their lives is not recorded, it is lost forever. Volunteer to help someone you love write an autobiography. If the person is quite old, you may want to interview them, recording their responses or taking notes, and then writing their autobiography entries for them.

23. **Write a biography of a relative or ancestor.** Have you heard stories about your great-grandmother and wished you could have known her? Do people still talk about Great Uncle Henry and his adventures, even though he's been dead for 50 years? Try collecting information about one of your ancestors or relatives. Besides factual information you can gather, like dates of birth, marriage, death, etc., see if you can collect photos of where they lived, their families, or anything else related to their lives. Interview those still living who knew them. What can they tell you about

the person? Try to write a biography that can be an accurate and interesting family keepsake.

24. **Create a family memory book.** Fill it with stories, family recipes, old photos, facts about your family, interesting trivia, and anything else you can think of. Do you have a coat of arms? If not, invent one that seems appropriate, or create a family logo that seems to represent what your family is like. Do you want to include a scrap of material from that special dress your grandma made for your fifth birthday? How about the letter your dad wrote to Santa when he was four? Do you have a copy of your uncle's essay that won first place in a county essay contest?

   Collect all the material you can find, and write appropriate explanations to go with the material. Give the book a title. (Since you may want to create new volumes every year or two, you may want to add "Volume I" to the name.)" You can have your book copied and bound at a photocopy center.

25. **Funnel your anger with a letter that requests a change**. Good old-fashioned letter writing is the perfect way to handle a situation that really makes you angry. Are you mad that your son's soccer team has three practices a week, instead of the one night promised? Write a letter to the coach suggesting a change. Are you irritated that the city council stopped funding your favorite local non-profit? Write a letter to council members. Are you fuming about being treated rudely at a local coffee shop? Write a letter to the store manager and suggest some training tips for employees. Besides being good writing practice, letters are generally more effective than phone calls because you can verbalize all of your thoughts without interruption. It's always great to be able to edit your thoughts, especially when you are angry.

Be sure to do more than complain. Tell what it is you want—a refund, a change in policy, an apology? Be specific.

When people take time to write letters, the letters are generally taken more seriously than angry phone calls or nasty confrontations. Also, letters printed, signed and sent through the mail are often more effective than e-mailed letters.

26. **Become a reviewer at Amazon.com**. Anyone can write a book review and post it at Amazon.com. It's easy, and others using the site find the reviews quite helpful. Simply go to www.amazon.com, find the book you want to review, and click on "Write a review." Be sure to read the reviewer guidelines first.

You may want to take it further and become a "Top Reviewer" by writing a lot of helpful, informative product reviews. When customers read a review on the web site, they have a chance to vote on whether or not they find the review helpful. Amazon tabulates the votes, and the people whose reviews are voted most helpful most often are selected as Top Reviewers. When a reviewer is designated a Top Reviewer, an icon appears by his or her name, with the reviewer's ranking (Top 1000 Reviewer, Top 500 Reviewer, Top 100 Reviewer, Top 50 Reviewer, Top 10 Reviewer, or #1 Reviewer.)

27. **Write a neighborhood newsletter.** Be the one to help bring your neighborhood closer. Collect news items from each family and put together a neighborhood newsletter. You might want to do it once or twice a year, once a month, or even more often. It may be difficult to collect news at first, but as people become accustomed to receiving the newsletter, they may start saving information for you. The newsletter might include a few travel photos from a neighbor's trip, a notice that a new babysitter on

the block is offering his or her services, news about a hospitalization, a new baby, a new puppy, etc.

28. **Go ahead and start that book you've always wanted to write.** Stop procrastinating. Just start. If you write regularly for even 15 minutes a day, you will make progress.

    To help keep you on track, you might want to join a writers' group, where you share your work regularly. You might want to subscribe to a writer's magazine, such as *The Writer* or *Writer's Digest*. You might want to find a writing "buddy"—someone you will "report" to on a regular basis, to share your work.

29. **Make a "word" poster as a gift for a friend or relative.** Start by collecting words and phrases that are special to you and the person who will receive the gift. For example, if you are making the poster for your best friend, you might list sentences and phrases that will recall memories: *Remember your true love, Charlie, in third grade?...The airport escalator escapade... hot fudge sundaes at Mulligan's...the prom dress sash falling in the toilet...Hank Wolfenbarger!...*

    After you have collected as many meaningful words, phrases, and sentences as possible, start your poster. Make it any size you want, but it's a good idea to use paper or poster board in a size standard for framing. (It's less expensive to use ready-made frames.) Use colored pencils, marking pens, or paints, and start writing in your words in different colors and sizes, and filling in with symbols like hearts, diamonds, or just colorful squiggles. Build your design as you go. On page 135 is just the top part of a word poster made by a woman for her friend Elaine.

    Another approach is to take advantage of the computer. Type all the words, phrases, and sentences in different colors, using various fonts and

sizes. Cut them out and create a collage, pasting all the items into a design. Take the collage to a photocopy center and have a color copy made. Frame it, and voila! You will have a gift that your friend or relative is sure to cherish.

30. **Write movie reviews.** After seeing a movie that you really loved or really hated, write a review, perhaps in the "thumbs up" or "thumbs down" style of reviewers Roger Ebert and Richard Roeper. Be sure to be specific. What exactly did you like? What exactly did you dislike? E-mail your reviews to your friends, even those who generally have different

movie tastes than you do. They will likely appreciate a movie review from a real person, especially if they receive it before they decide whether or not to see the movie.

31. **Create a cookbook.** If you like to cook, consider creating a cookbook, perhaps one with a specific theme: *Snacks Kids Can Make Themselves, Ruiz Family Recipes, Desserts for Chocoholics,* etc. A cookbook requires careful attention to instructions. Be sure to be as clear as possible about instructions, and be sure to include specific information about amounts. (Don't say, "two packages of green beans." Do you mean the 15 oz. size or the 32 oz. size?)

    Be sure to write an introduction for your cookbook. Tell why you chose the theme you did. Did you create the recipes yourself or collect them from various sources? What tips can you give, in general?

32. **Collect family stories.** What stories have been told and retold in your family over the years? Write them down for future generations.

    Have you grown up hearing about the time your grandfather received the sad news that an employee had died? He went to visit the widow to express his condolences. The poor woman listened and finally said, "I'm sorry, but he ain't dead yet!"

    Do your uncles and aunts laugh about the time they scared your mother half to death in church by slipping a rubber chicken in the pew as everyone stood to sing? When she turned to sit down after the hymn, she let out a scream that completely disrupted the service.

    Does everyone remember your brother's hideous and cheap car, the one he bought for next to nothing and everyone called the "Uncle Buckmobile," after the car in the movie *Uncle Buck*?

Write down all the family stories you can remember, and then get help from others as to details and specifics, as well as other stories you might have forgotten.

Of course, you will want to give a copy of your collection to all your family members.

33. **Create a family tree with a twist.** Make a family tree that has a story or anecdote beside each person's name and/or picture. For example, you might note under your grandmother's name the story you remember about how she had to go door-to-door as a child, selling buckets of honey. Or you could note by your brother's name the fact that he was born two months early and spent his first month of life in the hospital.

You might even make a humorous family tree, telling something funny about each person. You might even add special names, such as Patricia Ann "Gets Away with Murder" Freeman.

34. **Create the narration for a family video.** Collect family snapshots and have them put on videotape or DVD. Create a narration to go with them. What you say will be dictated by the pictures, your purpose, and your imagination. Do you want to create something funny, touching, informative, or beautiful? Write a narration that fits the mood you want to create.

35. **Write a class reunion book.** Volunteer to write a booklet for your class reunion, with stories about where graduates are now and what they are doing. If you are still in school, you might want to write a class memory book with stories of your current year in school.

36. **Imitate Charlie Bone.** In a book called *Midnight for Charlie Bone*, a boy named Charlie finds that he can look at photographs and hear conversations and thoughts that were taking place at the time the photo was taken. Imagine that you can do the same. Put together a collection of photos of your friends (or family) and write funny blurbs to go with each photo, showing what the people in the photograph are supposedly thinking, or telling what is *really* going on. Put up your display at a party or other get-together, to share with everyone.

37. **Make a slang dictionary.** Just for fun, if you are a young person, make a slang dictionary to give to your parents, with definitions to help them understand what kids are saying today. If you are a parent or grand-parent, write a slang dictionary with meanings of slang words from *your* generation, and share it with your children or grandchildren.

38. **Write a play and put it on.** Update a fairy tale and present it for kids at an elementary school. Reenact a piece of family history for a family reunion. Write a play that illustrates a moral for your Sunday school class. Write a skit that tells about someone's life, for that person's birthday party. There are countless possibilities for skits and plays.

39. **Make a gift of a personalized list.** For your very special grandfather, complete this sentence as many ways as possible: "A Grandpa Is..." List all the special things you appreciate about him. (Examples: A Grandpa Is...someone who never ever got tired of reading *Horton Hears a Who!* to me, even after he had already read it three times in one evening.) Of course, you might instead make a list for your grandmother, aunt, uncle, sister, brother, parent, or any other person who is special to you. Type up your list, and frame it as a gift. It is sure to be a cherished keep-sake.

40. **Put together a collection of stories on a theme.** Collect the stories from friends and/or relatives. Share your final collection with all who contribute. Just a few ideas for themes:

- escapades at summer camp
- horror stories about renovating a house
- stories about emergencies—the time you were snowbound, the time the electricity went out, the time the tornado hit town
- stories about junior/senior prom
- adventures at the mall
- stories about unexpected visitors (human or non-human)
- sports adventures

41. **Write a guide for how to do something.** The subject depends, of course, on what you know how to do. Think outside the box. Maybe you want to write a guide to navigating the subway system in your city, for friends or relatives coming to visit. Maybe you want to write a "How to Use Google" "Or How to Buy Things on E-Bay" guide for a grandparent or great-grandparent new to the Internet. Maybe you want to write down, for future generations, instructions for a disappearing art or skill, like "How to Make Dill Pickles" or "How to Make Soap."

42. **Create a personalized calendar.** In addition to pictures or photographs for each month, add anecdotes on special dates throughout the year. (Example: February 12, Allyssa's birthday. Remember the time she threw a temper tantrum when she couldn't sleep in Grandma's laundry basket? Poor baby!)

43. **Write a history of family flops.** Every family has them—stories of family flops, mistakes, disasters, goofs. Write them down for your "Family

Flop" book. Do you laugh about the time your mom's beer cheese soup smelled so much like dirty feet that she had to throw it out? Or the time your dad got so mad teaching your brother to drive that he got out of the Jeep and started kicking the tires and swearing? Or the time you went to Aunt Mabel's for Thanksgiving dinner, and she was just putting the 20-pound turkey in the oven when you arrived. ("I'm running a little late," she said.)

Family flop stories—maybe even with some cartoon illustrations—can make a great gift to share.

44. **Create a "most wanted" poster featuring your friends.** Take front and side views of each person. Underneath each photo, tell what each is "wanted" for. (Examples: Joe Proust—Didn't put the proper header on his paper for picky Miss Clarkson...Jennifer Garcia—Wore her sister's favorite top, without asking permission, and dripped spaghetti sauce down the front.)

45. **Keep an e-mail journal.** Find a writing partner and make a commitment to write a little or a lot to each other every single day. Send your observations and reflections to each other through e-mail. After a few months or a year, compile all the e-mails you have received into one document and send it back to the original writer. That person then does the same for you. This is an easy way to capture a day-to-day memoir.

46. **Start your own blog on a subject.** Many have feared that technology would bring about the end of books and writing. However, in a strange twist, technology has opened up an entirely new realm of writing and expression—blogging. A blog (short for *web log*) is part memoir, part journalism, part personal diary, part graffiti and part op-ed piece. It is very personal, while still being very public.

Blogging offers the same benefits of journaling, but it is interactive. While journaling is a traditionally private way to practice writing, blogging gives you the same practice while also giving you direct interaction with a reading audience. It provides the perfect opportunity to flex and exercise your writing muscles.

Before you begin a blog of your own, read a variety of blogs. There are blogs for just about every imaginable subject—knitting, immigration, home-schooling, Harry Potter, Wal-Mart, you name it. Many of them allow you to submit your own thoughts or comments with a simple click of the button. To find a number of blogs, visit www.blogger com.

Then start your own blog. At www.blogger.com, there is no cost involved. While some well-known writers and journalists dabble in blogging, most bloggers are unknown. You have as much chance of being read as anyone else in the world!

47. **Publish poetry on the web.** When was the last time you bought a book of poetry? Many people seem to love poetry, but very few people ever spend money for poetry books. For this reason, publishers generally spend very little of their publishing budget on poetry books, and bookstores generally give them only a small amount of shelf space. The Internet, however, provides a relatively inexpensive way to publish and share poetry with the world.

Give it a try. You can create your own poetry web site and even ask for reader feedback. Or you can also seek out poetry blogs, which allow poets from all over the world to enter poems and receive feedback.

48. **Start a family or personal web site.** Your Internet provider most likely has web space included with your monthly membership. Take advantage of it by creating a web site. What can you put on a personal or family web site? There is no end to the possibilities. Here are just a few of them:

- Use it as a way to share your children with grandparents or other family members who live far away. Dazzle them with photos, movies and scanned children's artwork. Exercise your writing muscles by including stories, musings and quips about your kids.

- Use it to post highlights and photos of a trip or vacation. Have you ever had to squirm through someone's boring vacation slides? Or page through endless books of photos? The Internet provides a better way to share. Use a web site to tell friends and family about your trip. Upload photos from your digital camera, and take the opportunity to practice writing with stories about the touching, humorous and disastrous parts of your vacation. Friends and relatives can go to the web site for either a quick or a leisurely tour whenever they wish.

- Use it to share your knowledge and enthusiasm about a hobby or interest. You can write about the pastime you love most—hunting, building doll houses, raising turtles, baking, etc. Your hobby-based web site can include personal experience stories, your own expert tips and advice, book and product reviews, and/or personal thoughts and musings.

- Use it to further a cause. The Internet is a great way to reach out to others. You can use a web site to connect, motivate and share. You can write about something you care deeply about, with the possibility of reaching a large audience. A web site devoted to your cause can include poignant stories, inspirational thoughts, summaries, comments, and narratives about your personal experience.

49. **Plan the vacation or trip you intend to take someday.** Where is it you fully intend to go, someday? Have you always dreamed of spending a month in Paris? Going on a safari to Africa? Touring Australia? Start a notebook, planning your trip and describing what you want to do.

    Don't plan the trip you know will never take place. If you have absolutely no faith at all that you will ever spend a year sailing around the world, don't write about that trip. If, however, you think there's a good chance, if everything goes right, that you will someday sail a boat in the Greek Isles, that's the trip to start bringing to life in your imagination.

    After your notebook is well underway, share it with the person you would like to share the trip with. What would that person like to add to the trip? What good ideas can he or she add? Keep amending your notebook until you have described your perfect journey. Don't be surprised if the act of planning it helps create the circumstances that will make it a reality!

50. **Write a short documentary film.** What subject is near and dear to your heart? What would you like others to know more about? Write a script for a short documentary film on the subject. Film it yourself with a video camera, or find a partner to do the filming. Then make arrangements for others to see your film.

* * * * *

About the Authors

Dawn DiPrince teaches specialty writing classes to elementary and middle school students and memoir writing classes to senior adults. She is the founder of *BlueSky Quarterly,* a magazine that celebrates life in southeastern Colorado. She lives in Pueblo, Colorado, with her husband and two young children.

Cheryl Miller Thurston taught English and writing classes for more than 13 years, grades seven through university level. She is the author of many plays, musicals, and books for teachers. She lives with her husband and pampered cat in Loveland, Colorado.

Cottonwood Press, Inc.
1-800-864-4297
www.cottonwoodpress.com
Visit our web site for a complete product list.